Published by www.lulu.com

This book has been endorsed by OCR for use with the OCR GCSE Computing specification.

Many thanks to:

- OCR for their feedback on Edition 1, which has directly contributed to the changes made.
- Dave Adams at OCR for sorting out the slight blurring on some of my diagrams in Edition 1.

Whilst I have made every effort to ensure that the contents of this book are accurate and true, I will not be held liable either directly or indirectly for any omissions, mistakes or oversights herein. I welcome and encourage comments and suggestions for future editions.

Important Copyright Information

About the author, Susan Robson

I have a degree in Computer Science from Manchester University, a PGCE from Portsmouth University and a certificate that says I can swim two lengths (good news when I get out of my depth!!).

I worked for International Computers Ltd (pre Fujisu days) straight out of university followed by 12 years in technical pre-sales and then sales for ECI Telecom. In my mid-thirties I decided I needed a career change and moved into teaching Computing at Queen Mary's Sixth Form College, Basingstoke. I am currently Head of Computing at Bedales in Petersfield where I teach OCR's GCSE Computing and OCR's A Level Computing.

Feedback to the author at: **susanjrobson@gmail.com**

TABLE OF CONTENTS

CHAPTER 1:   FUNDAMENTALS OF COMPUTER SYSTEMS

This topic is about developing a mental model of a computer system in terms of its key components.

BASIC COMPUTER SYSTEM MODEL

The OCR Specification says that you should be able to:

- define a computer system

A computer system is made up of hardware and software. Hardware is any physical component that makes up the computer. Software is any program that runs on the computer.

Computers systems are all around us. They are not just the PCs on the desk but include mobile phones, cash machines, supermarket tills and the engine management systems in a modern-day car. The diagram to the right shows the basic model of a computer system.

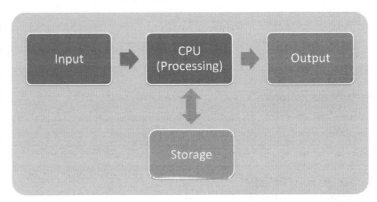

All computer systems must have **input devices** that get data from the real-world. This could be a mouse and keyboard on a conventional PC but could be a temperature sensor (thermistor) in a commercial greenhouse or the microphone on a mobile phone. Input devices take real-world data and convert it into a form that can be stored on the computer. More details on this in Chapter 2, "Data Representation".

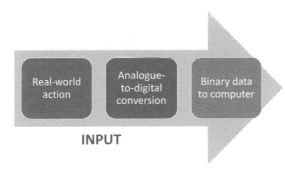

The input from these devices is processed and the computer system will generate outputs. The **output device** could be a conventional computer screen or it could be a motor that opens a greenhouse window or the speaker that produces sound on a phone.

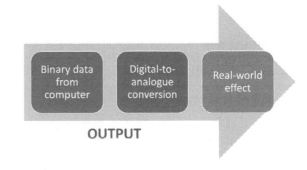

The forth component is **storage**. The computer system may need to use stored data to perform the processing and, as a result of processing input, may generate data that is then stored.

Any computer system will have these four basic components. These components will be discussed in more detail in Chapter 3, "Hardware".

IMPORTANCE OF COMPUTERS

The OCR Specification says that you should be able to:

- describe the importance of computer systems in the modern world
- explain the need for reliability in computer systems

Think about all of the places you go in the course of a day and all the computer systems you see. Computers are embedded in household appliances such as fridges and microwave ovens. Your mobile phone is a computer system, your TV and games console are too. When you go home the car has a computer controlling the engine as well as the car's GPS and stereo being computer systems.

We are becoming increasingly dependent on computer systems at school, at work and at home. Consider what problems you would have if all of these computers stopped working! If the games console didn't work you might be upset but it wouldn't be a big problem. If the network at school went down you wouldn't be able to get to any of the resources and teachers wouldn't be able to show you their slides or use smart-whiteboards. If there are problems with computers systems in shops they can't sell anything and if bank systems have problems people cannot access their money, or worse still, other people can!

??? For you to find out...

Look at some news websites to find stories about computer systems failures.

If computer-controlled signage on motorways goes wrong there could be health and safety implications. If computer systems in hospitals go wrong people could die. The **reliability** of computer systems is extremely important. In some situations it is more important than how quickly they work or how many features they have.

Measuring Reliability

How do you know how reliable a computer system is? We talk about system **availability** meaning how long it is available for. For example, if a system is down (unavailable) for 1 hour in a 100 hour period, then the system availability is 99% for this period. Normally equipment manufacturers will quote average availability over a long period of time.

Another way of measuring a system's reliability is to measure the length of time between system failures. **MTBF** is the Mean Time Between Failure and is quoted by equipment manufacturers as an indication of reliability.

Protecting Against System Failures

If a computer system's reliability is very important then a company may need to have spare hardware in place just in case of system failures. **Hardware redundancy** is one way to protect systems. This means having more than one of a critical component. For example, the computers in a commercial aeroplane will all have backup computers to take their place if they go wrong.

> **??? For you to find out...**
>
> Look up "RAID computer storage" to see how companies protect their computer systems against disk failure.

If software or hardware problems occur, the data is most at risk. This will be stored on a disk on a server somewhere. As well as redundant hardware companies must make sure that data is backed up regularly.

Sometimes computer systems are so important to a company that they cannot function without them. A computer system failure could mean that a company goes out of business in just a few days. **Disaster recovery** plans are sometimes put in place so a company can switch over to a complete, new system with all their own data on it, often with hours. There are disaster recovery companies that specialise in offering this service to companies who depend on their computer systems.

PROFESSIONAL STANDARDS

> The OCR Specification says that you should be able to:
>
> - explain the need for adherence to suitable professional standards in the development, use and maintenance of computer systems

Computer systems are complex. If everyone involved in creating, using and maintaining a system did things their own way it would make it even more complicated. Professional standards can be formally agreed or "de facto" ("de" is pronounced "day").

De facto standards are when lots of people start working in a certain way and more people think it looks like a good idea and start doing it that way as well. Over time, this way of working becomes a standard, just because that is how most people do it. It is not a formally agreed standard where a committee of people sit down and agree how something should be done.

Professional Standards in System Development

There are several approaches, or models, that define how a computer system is developed. Any new system starts with an idea or a need that must be analysed so a system can be designed and created. This development may take many months or years so there needs to be a way of splitting this down into logical steps and defining what each step will involve.

One such model is the "Waterfall Model". This model defines definite steps that are completed one at a time to guide the process from beginning to end. Each step has specific outputs that lead into the next step. You can return to a previous stage if necessary but you then have to work back down through the following stages.

Another model is "Rapid Application Development" (RAD), where the client is much more involved in the process. This method starts with a prototype that is developed gradually into a full solution with customer feedback at each stage.

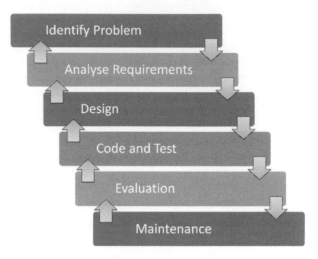

These are both standard approaches that teams of developers would be familiar with. Professionals in the industry would be familiar with these standard frameworks. They wouldn't have to learn a new methodology every time they move to another job.

Professional Standards in Coding

De facto standards in programming include the use of:

- Indents to clearly show where sections of code are inside a construct such as a loop
- Comments in code to outline the algorithm and define the purpose of each part of the program
- Meaningful identifiers so anyone can read the code and understand it, for example "Total" instead of "X"

These are all considered "good practice", the best way to do something.

Using professional standards also means that programmers do not plagiarise other people's work. When developers write the programs they create something from their own mind. This is referred to as "intellectual property". The Copyright, Designs and Patents Act protects people's intellectual property rights. It protects the fact that they have worked hard to create something and stops somebody else just using it for their own gain. The "Federation Against Software Theft" (FAST) attempts to enforce the copyright laws and protect programmers' rights.

However, some developers prefer not to protect their work in this way. Instead they actively collaborate with other programmers and create Open Source code, which others can use at no cost. The professional standards applied here are that any new code created from open source code is then also shared as open source code. ("Open Source" is discussed in more detail in Chapter 4, "Software").

Professional Standards in Documentation

Professional standards apply to documentation as well as coding. A system developer will document the system using standard diagrams. These diagrams all use recognised sets of symbols.

While studying this GCSE you will use system flow charts (see Chapter 7, "Programming") to design algorithms. The symbols used in these diagrams are industry standard. You will also draw logic diagrams using standard symbols for the NOT, AND and OR logic gates.

These standards mean that system developers can:

- Work in teams to develop a system because they all have a common understanding of the design tools and diagrams.
- Move between companies because the standards apply across the whole industry.
- Pick up someone else's design and code the program to achieve it.
- Maintain somebody else's program when the customer's requirements change.

Professional Standards for Health and Safety

Where the safety of people is concerned there needs to be more than just a de facto standard. There are laws that protect people and define standards for how computers systems should be used. For example, the Health & Safety at Work Act includes Display Screen Regulations. When developing a computer system the use of the system on a day-to-day basis must be considered. Developers design systems to meet health and safety regulations.

CONSIDERATIONS WHEN CREATING COMPUTER SYSTEMS

The OCR Specification says that you should be able to:

- explain the importance of ethical, environmental and legal considerations when creating computer systems

When creating a computer system the designer will take into account the system requirements, the money available and the timescales it has to be produced in.

There are also legal, ethical and environmental considerations that will affect the system's design.

Legal Considerations

When a computer system is designed and implemented it must meet legal requirements. Some of the laws that system designers should consider are as follows:

- **The Data Protection Act** says that anyone who stores personal details must keep them secure. Companies with computer systems that store any personal data must have processes and security mechanisms designed into the system to meet this requirement.

- **The Health and Safety at Work Act** makes employers responsible for their staff. Design considerations should provide appropriate working conditions for staff. Designers should consider how easy systems will be to use and any health implications there might be based on their choices of software, screen layout, input methods and the hardware used.

- **The Copyright, Designs and Patents Act** makes it illegal to use software without buying the appropriate licenses. When a computer system is designed and implemented licensing must be considered in terms of which software should be used. Is Open Source the way to go or is the cost of proprietary software worth it in the long run?

Ethical Considerations

Ethical considerations are all about fairness. When creating a computer system a company should consider fairness. This may impact where call centres are located and where programming work is done. Examples of ethical issues around computer systems are:

- Is it fair that some people cannot afford computers?
- Are countries like India being exploited as a source of cheap labour for call centres and for programming?
- Should companies use local programmers and call centres?
- Does the system design disadvantage some part of the community?
- Does the system design promote accessibility for all?

Environmental Considerations

Environmental issues include the carbon footprint and waste products that result from manufacturing computer systems but this is often outweighed by the positive effects on the environment of using computerised systems to manage processes that might otherwise generate more pollution.

Consideration may include:

- Does a computer system mean that people can work from home and therefore drive less?
- Does a computer system mean more manufacturing?
- Is working at home more environmentally friendly than everyone working in a big office, in terms of heating and lighting?
- Do computer-managed engines work more efficiently? Less pollution and use less fuel?

GLOSSARY OF TERMS

Basic Model

Computer System	A combination of hardware and software components that allow input, processing and output of data.
Hardware	The physical components that make up a computer system.
Software	The programs that run on a computer system.
Input Devices	Hardware devices that take real-world analogue data and convert it into a digital form that can be stored on a computer. For example: keyboard, mouse, microphone, webcam, scanner, sensors.
Output Device	Hardware devices that use digital data from a computer to produce a form that is understandable to a person. For example: monitors, printers, speakers, projectors, actuators (motors).

Importance of Computers

Reliability	How much you can depend on the computer system being available when you need it. Usually measured in terms of availability.
Availability	The proportion of time that a system is operational, usually expressed as a percentage over a certain period of time. For example, 95% measured over 1 year.
MTBF	Mean Time Between Failure: a measure of availability often quoted by hardware manufacturers. For example 2.56 years between failures means that, on average, the hardware can be expected to last 2.56 years before it goes wrong.
Redundancy	Spare hardware components are built into a system so, in the event of a component failing, the system can swap over to the spare one. *(Discussed in Chapter 6, "Networks")*
Disaster Recovery	Where a company has plans to replace a system quickly if there is a catastrophe (fire, flood, bomb etc). Designed to minimise the time the system is down. *(Discussed in Chapter 6, "Networks")*

From the specimen paper

1. An advertisement for a personal computer is shown below.

av systems
T-800 DELUXE

Ultra-fast QUAL processor
4GB RAM
320GB Hard Drive
DP Premier Home Edition
64-Bit operating system
+   PS Anti-Virus
CCS Graphix 3.0
WolfWeb High-Speed
Internet

(a) (i) What is software?

   Programs that run on a computer.   [1]

   (ii) Give one example of software from the advertisement.

   PS Anti-Virus   [1]

(b)   The table below contains a list of hardware devices.
      Tick one box in each row to show what type of device it is.
      The first one has been done for you.

Hardware device	Input	Output	Processing	Storage	Communication
Monitor		✓			
CPU			✓		
Mouse	✓				
DVD-Drive				✓	
Speakers		✓			

                                                                              [4]

CHAPTER 2: DATA REPRESENTATION IN COMPUTERS

This topic is all about how data is stored in a computer. Data can be in a number of different formats. In this chapter you will learn how computers store numbers, text, images, sounds and program instructions.

UNITS

The OCR Specification says that you should be able to:

- define the terms bit, nibble, byte, kilobyte, megabyte, gigabyte, terabyte
- understand that data need to be converted into a binary format to be processed by a computer

Computers are made up of complicated hardware that stores and processes data. If you break a computer down into its most basic components you have millions of circuits that either allow electricity to flow, or not. Imagine a whole row of light switches that you can switch on and off in different combinations to mean different things. Each switch is either on or off. It only has two states. That is why everything stored in a computer can be stored as a series of 1s and 0s. This is called *binary*.

A single **1** or **0** is a **b**inary dig**it**, or a *bit* for short. A group of eight bits is called a *byte*.

Imagine you've taken a small bite out of an apple, you might call that a nibble. So four bits, half a byte, is called a *nibble*!

Just as a kilometer is 1000 meters, we can group together 1024 bytes and call it a *kilobyte*.

8 bits	=	1 *byte*
1024 bytes	=	1 *kilobyte*
1024 kilobytes	=	1 *megabyt*e
1024 megabytes	=	1 *gigabyte*
1024 gigabytes	=	1 *terabyte*

??? For you to find out...

1. Why isn't a kilobyte 1000 bytes? 1024 seems a strange number. How does it relate to binary?

2. What comes after terabytes?

NUMBERS

The OCR Specification says that you should be able to:

• convert positive denary whole numbers (0-255) into 8-bit binary numbers and vice versa

Imagine you are back in primary school, learning to add again. 7+5 = 12, write down the 2 units but carry the group of 10. 23 would be 2 groups of 10 and 3 units.

Counting in binary is the same except instead of digits 0 to 9 we only have two digits, 1 and 0, so we carry the group of 2. In maths we call this Base 2. This is how we count to 10 in binary:

denary	binary	
0	0	
1	1	
2	10	Notice that we now go to the second column – one group of 2, no units
3	11	One group of 2 plus one unit 2+1=3
4	100	Now we go to the third column, 2 groups of previous column, so this is 4
5	101	
6	110	
7	111	
8	1000	Every time we go to the next column it is two times the previous column!
9	1001	
10	1010	

Can you see the pattern? The column headings in a binary number double each time:

	x 2		x 2		x 2		x 2		x 2		x 2		x 2	

128	64	32	16	8	4	2	1
2x2x2x2x2x2x2	2x2x2x2x2x2	2x2x2x2x2	2x2x2x2	2x2x2	2x2	2	1
2^7	2^6	2^5	2^4	2^3	2^2	2^1	1^0

To convert the binary number 111001 into a denary (decimal or base 10) number use the column headings. The number below is 32+16+8+1 = 57 (add up the column headings where there is a 1).

128	64	32	16	8	4	2	1
0	0	1	1	1	0	0	1

To convert a denary number to a binary number, use the same column headings. You need to find the biggest column heading that you can take away from the number and start there:

Let's convert 57 into binary:

- The biggest column heading we can take out of 57 is 32 (the next one is 64, which is too big).

- Write a 1 under column heading 32. That leaves us with 57 – 32 = 25.

  - Write a 1 under the column heading 16 (because we can take 16 out of 25). 25 – 16 leaves 9

    - You should be able to see now that 9 is an 8 and a 1 so we end up with:

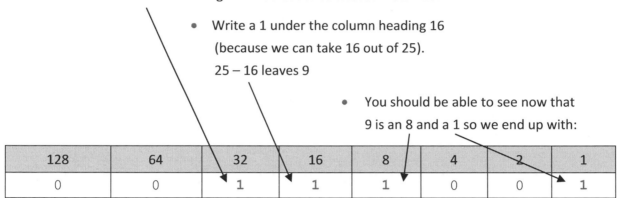

128	64	32	16	8	4	2	1
0	0	1	1	1	0	0	1

Always double check by adding the columns up at the end. They should give you the number you started with! 32+16+8+1 = 57 ✓

Here are some more examples:

Denary	Binary							
	128	64	32	16	8	4	2	1
23	0	0	0	1	0	1	1	1
84	0	1	0	1	0	1	0	0
255	1	1	1	1	1	1	1	1

So far we have only looked at numbers using eight columns. This is an 8-bit number, or a byte.

00000011 is binary for 3 but so is 11. You do not need the leading zeros for it to be a valid number but we tend to write groups of 8 bits because computers usually store data in bytes.

!!! NB…

255 is a significant number in binary, it will come up a lot in other parts of the course!

What do you notice about the number 255 in binary?

Obviously numbers can be bigger than 255 but in computers we need to represent data in a specific number of bits. For example, in Delphi programs an integer is always stored in 16 bits (2 bytes) whereas a real number is stored in 4 bytes.

At GCSE level you will only need to work with 8-bit numbers!

The OCR Specification says that you should be able to:

- add two 8-bit binary integers and explain overflow errors which may occur

Adding binary works in exactly the same way as adding denary numbers except you carry groups of 2 instead of groups of 10:

Adding denary	Adding binary

1 2 3 4 5
  1 3 4 +
1 2 4 7 9
 	
7 8 2 3 5
  $_1$9$_1$7 +
7 8 3 3 2
 	
Notice that you carry 1 when you get to ten in a column so 5+7=12, write 2 in that column but carry one group of ten.
	1 0 0 1 0
	  1 0 1 +
	1 0 1 1 1
	
	1 0 0 1 1
	  $_1$1$_1$1$_1$1 +
	1 1 0 1 0
	
	Notice that you carry 1 when you get to two in a column so 1+1=2, write 0 in that column but carry one group of two.
	In the second column, 1+1+1=3, a group of two to carry but 1 unit in that column!

Some more examples:

```
1 0 1 0 1 1 0 0          0 0 1 0 1 1 0 1          0 0 1 0 1 1 0 1
0 0 0 1 0 0 0 1 +        1 0 0 0 0 1 0 1 +        1 0 0 0 0 1 1 1 +
1 0 1 1 1 1 0 1          1 0 1 1 0 0 1 0          1 0 1 1 0 1 0 0
```

The biggest number you can represent with 8 bits is 255 (128+64+32+16+8+4+2+1).

If you add two binary numbers together that result in a number bigger than 255, it will need 9 bits. A computer stores things in memory in a finite amount of space. If you cannot represent the number in that amount of space because it is too big, then we get **overflow**.

For example:

```
( 2 5 2 )    1 1 1 1 1 1 0 0
( 1 5 )      0 0 0 0 1 1 1 1 +
( 2 6 7 )   1 0 0 0 0 1 0 1 1
```

The computer would need 9 bits to represent 267 so this 9th bit doesn't fit in the byte allocated. This is overflow.

??? **For you to find out...**

What is the biggest decimal number you can store using:

- 4 bits?
- 2 bytes?

The OCR Specification says that you should be able to:

- convert positive denary integers (0-255) into 2-digit hexadecimal numbers and vice versa
- convert between binary and hexadecimal equivalents of the same number
- explain the use of hexadecimal numbers to represent binary numbers

Which of these is easier to remember: **0 1 0 1 1 0 1 1** or **5 B**? Humans are not very good at remembering long strings of numbers so, to make it easier for us, we can represent every group of 4 bits (a nibble) with a single digit.

The smallest value you can have with 4 bits is 0000. The largest value is 1111. This means that we need to represent the denary values 0 to 15 with a single digit. The trouble is, we only have numerical digits 0 to 9! To get around this problem we use letters to fill the gap until we get to 16.

This is called Base 16 in Maths, or **hexadecimal** in Computing. We abbreviate this to **hex**.

This is how we count to 16 in denary, binary and hex:

denary	binary	Hex
0	0	0
1	1	1
2	10	2
3	11	3
4	100	4
5	101	5
6	110	6
7	111	7
8	1000	8
9	1001	9
10	1010	A
11	1011	B
12	1100	C
13	1101	D
14	1110	E
15	1111	F
16	1 0000	10
255	1111 1111	FF

??? For you to find out...

How is hex used to code colours in HTML (web pages)? For example, what colour is #FF00FF?

Search on "Color palette hex" and see what you can find out.

A single Hex digit replaces 4 bits.

15 is the biggest number you can have with 4 bits so 16 is one group of 16 and no units (just like we did before with binary).

255 is 15 groups of 16 + 15 units ie: (15 x 16) + 15

To Convert a Binary Number to Hex:

In GCSE Computing you will only need to work with 8-bit binary numbers, which can be represented as two hex digits. The first hex digit represents groups of 16, the second hex digit represents the units left over.

```
92 in denary   =   0 1 0 1  1 1 0 0   = 5C in hex
                        5         12      (12 is replaced by C)
                   (groups of 16)  (units)
```

To Convert a Denary Number to Hex:

To convert 182 in denary into hex the first step is to work out how many groups of 16 there are in 182. Secondly work out how many units are left over.

182 / 16 = 11 remainder 6

11 is B in hex. 6 is just 6!   So   182 denary = B6 hex

Alternatively, you can convert the denary to binary first and then convert the binary to hex, as above.

CHARACTERS

The OCR Specification says that you should be able to:

- explain the use of binary codes to represent characters
- explain the term character set
- describe with examples (for example ASCII and Unicode) the relationship between the number of bits per character in a character set and the number of characters which can be represented

Every time a character is typed on a keyboard a code number is transmitted to the computer. The code numbers are stored in binary. Different sets of codes are available for different types of computer. PCs use a **character set** called **ASCII**, American Standard Code for Information Interchange. A character set is the group of characters that can be coded.

The next page shows a version of ASCII that uses 7 bits to code each character. The biggest number you can have with seven bits is 1111111 in binary (127 in denary). The smallest number you can have with seven bits is 0000000 (0 in denary!). This means that you can have 128 different characters in the character set (using codes 0 to 127).

Other character encoding systems include:

- **Unicode**: A 16-bit encoding system that has 2^{16} (65,536) different characters in its character set.
- **EBCDIC** *(pronounced eb-sid-ic)*: Extended Binary Coded Decimal Interchange Code, an 8-bit encoding system that has 2^8 (255) different characters in its character set.

7-bit ASCII Table

ASCII	DEC	Binary	ASCII	DEC	Binary	ASCII	DEC	Binary	ASCII	DEC	Binary
NULL	000	000 0000	space	032	010 0000	@	064	100 0000	`	096	110 0000
SOH	001	000 0001	!	033	010 0001	A	065	10 00001	a	097	110 0001
STX	002	000 0010	"	034	010 0010	B	066	100 0010	b	098	110 0010
ETX	003	000 0011	#	035	010 0011	C	067	100 0011	c	099	110 0011
EOT	004	000 0100	$	036	010 0100	D	068	100 0100	d	100	110 0100
ENQ	005	000 0101	%	037	010 0101	E	069	100 0101	e	101	110 0101
ACK	006	000 0110	&	038	010 0110	F	070	100 0110	f	102	110 0110
BEL	007	000 0111	'	039	010 0111	G	071	100 0111	g	103	110 0111
BS	008	000 1000	(	040	010 1000	H	072	100 1000	h	104	110 1000
HT	009	000 1001	)	041	010 1001	I	073	100 1001	i	105	110 1001
LF	010	000 1010	*	042	010 1010	J	074	100 1010	j	106	110 1010
VT	011	000 1011	+	043	010 1011	K	075	100 1011	k	107	110 1011
FF	012	000 1100	,	044	010 1100	L	076	100 1100	l	108	110 1100
CR	013	000 1101	–	045	010 1101	M	077	100 1101	m	109	110 1101
SO	014	000 1110	.	046	010 1110	N	078	100 1110	n	110	110 1110
SI	015	000 1111	/	047	010 1111	O	079	100 1111	o	111	110 1111
DLE	016	001 0000	0	048	011 0000	P	080	101 0000	p	112	111 0000
DC1	017	001 0001	1	049	011 0001	Q	081	101 0001	q	113	111 0001
DC2	018	001 0010	2	050	011 0010	R	082	101 0010	r	114	111 0010
DC3	019	001 0011	3	051	011 0011	S	083	101 0011	s	115	111 0011
DC4	020	001 0100	4	052	011 0100	T	084	101 0100	t	116	111 0100
NAK	021	001 0101	5	053	011 0101	U	085	101 0101	u	117	111 0101
SYN	022	001 0110	6	054	011 0110	V	086	101 0110	v	118	111 0110
ETB	023	001 0111	7	055	011 0111	W	087	101 0111	w	119	111 0111
CAN	024	001 1000	8	056	011 1000	X	088	101 1000	x	120	111 1000
EM	025	001 1001	9	057	011 1001	Y	089	101 1001	y	121	111 1001
SUB	026	001 1010	:	058	011 1010	Z	090	101 1010	z	122	111 1010
ESC	027	001 1011	;	059	011 1011	[	091	101 1011	{	123	111 1011
FS	028	001 1100	<	060	011 1100	\	092	101 1100			124	111 1100
GS	029	001 1101	=	061	011 1101	]	093	101 1101	}	125	111 1101
RS	030	001 1110	>	062	011 1110	^	094	101 1110	~	126	111 1110
US	031	001 1111	?	063	011 1111	_	095	101 1111	DEL	127	111 1111

The characters are in numerical sequence, ie: if "A" is 65 then "C" must be 67. Also, they have an order so you can says that "7"<"9" and that "a">"A".

IMAGES

The OCR Specification says that you should be able to:

- explain the representation of an image as a series of pixels represented in binary
- explain the need for metadata to be included in the file such as height, width and colour depth
- discuss the effect of colour depth and resolution on the size of an image file

Images can be stored in different ways on a computer. When you create a drawing in PowerPoint this is a vector graphic. It is made up of lines with specific properties such as line style, line colour, where it starts and where it ends. The computer stores all of this data about each line in binary.

When you take a photograph on a digital camera it is not made up of lines. The picture somehow has to capture the continuously changing set of colours and shades that make up the real-life view. To store this type of image on a computer the image is broken down into very small elements called pixels. A **pixel** (short for picture element) is one specific colour. The whole image may be 600 pixels wide by 400 pixels deep (just an example). 600 x 400 is referred to as the picture's **resolution**. If the resolution of a picture is increased, then more pixels will need to be stored. This increases the size of the image file.

Making an image file

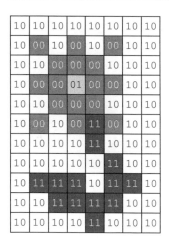

For this picture of a flower I will use 4 colours. I therefore need 2 bits to record the colour of each pixel:

11	10	01	00

The number of bits used to store each pixel dictates how many colours a picture can contain. 8 bits per pixel will give 256 possible colours. The number of bits per pixel is referred to as the **colour depth**.

If the colour depth is increased so more bits are used to represent each pixel, then the overall size of the file will increase.

If I record the value of each pixel in a file starting from the top left-hand corner and going left to right across each row I would end up with the following data file:

```
10 10 10 10 10 10 10 10 10 00 10 00 10 00 10 10 10 10 00
00 00 10 10 10 10 00 00 01 00 00 10 10 10 10 00 00 00 10
10 10 10 00 10 00 11 00 10 10 10 10 10 11 10 10 10 etc
```

For the computer to interpret this file and rebuild the picture it must know some other things about this data file. For example, the picture's resolution is 8x11 pixels, the colour depth is 2 bits per pixel. Data about the data file itself is called **metadata**.

SOUND

The OCR Specification says that you should be able to:

- explain how sound can be sampled and stored in digital form
- explain how sampling intervals and other considerations affect the size of a sound file and the quality of its playback

Sound waves are **analogue**, which means continuously changing. Anything stored on a computer has to be stored as a series of binary numbers, **digital**. To store sound on a computer we need to convert the waveform into a numerical representation. The device that takes real-world analogue signals and converts them to a digital representation is called an Analogue-to-Digital converter (**ADC**).

For sound waves, the analogue signal is converted as follows:

- Measure the amplitude (height of wave) at regular intervals (sampling)
- Store the values as a series of binary numbers in a file

1	0.8
2	2.0
3	3.4
4	5.0
5	6.6
6	8.1
7	10.0
8	12.0
9	14.0
10	16.0
11	17.4
12	18.0
13	17.8
14	17.2
15	15.5
16	13.8
17	11.6
18	8.4
19	5.3
20	3.0
21	1.7
22	1.0
23	1.2
24	2.0
25	3.2
26	4.6
27	7.0
28	9.0
29	11.0
30	12.0

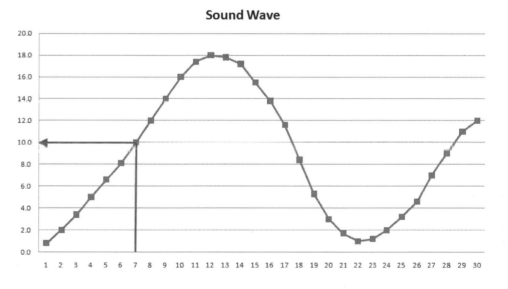

Sound Quality is affected by:

Sample Resolution: The number of bits used to store each sample.
The more bits used the better the accuracy of the sound file.

Sample Interval: The time period between taking samples/measurements.
The more frequently the sound is sampled, the better the quality of playback.

Synthesis:

Sound **synthesis** is when the sound is re-created by the computer through speakers from this file.

INSTRUCTIONS

The OCR Specification says that you should be able to:

- explain how instructions are coded as bit patterns
- explain how the computer distinguishes between instructions and data

Computer programs are made up of instructions. If you write a program in Delphi, for example, you use commands like `write` and `read`. As we have already established, the computer will represent these in binary to store them. When you **compile** and run your program the computer converts the high level programming language into **machine code**, which is a binary representation of the instructions you typed.

Instruction Set

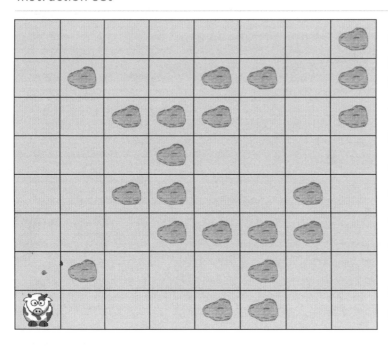

Clarence the cow needs to graze all of the grassy squares but avoid the ones with the rocks in.

The **instruction set** for this children's game has the following commands:

- RIGHT: Turn 90° to the right
- MOVE: Move forward one square
- EAT: Eat the grass in this square
- REV: Move backwards one square

Using these commands Clarence can traverse the board, eating the grass.

This instruction set only contains four instructions so the computer could represent each command with a sequence of two bits as shown here.

The group of bits that represents the instruction (or operation) is called the **op-code**. If a particular processor had an instruction set that used 8 bits for the op-code, then there could be as many as 256 different instructions.

RIGHT	00
MOVE	01
EAT	10
REV	11

The data used by the program is also in binary so the computer needs to tell the difference between bits that represent programs and bits that represent data. This is where the operating system comes in. Essentially, every location in memory has a unique **address** (a location number). The operating system knows where the data and the programs are located in main memory. (See Chapter 4, "Software").

GLOSSARY OF TERMS

Units

Bit	A single binary digit: 1 or 0
Byte	8 bits
Nibble	4 bits
Kilobyte	1024 bytes / 2^{10} bytes
Megabyte	1024 kilobytes / 2^{20} bytes
Gigabyte	1024 megabytes / 2^{30} bytes
Terabyte	1024 gigabytes / 2^{40} bytes

Numbers

Binary	Base 2 number system, used by computers, uses the digits 1 & 0 only.
Denary	Base 10 number system, how we normally count, uses digits 0 to 9.
Hexadecimal (hex)	Base 16 number system used by humans to represent groups of four bits at a time. Uses digits 0 to F.
Overflow	When the result of a numeric calculation is too large to be stored in the space reserved for that type of data.

Characters

Character set	The set of symbols that can be represented by a computer. The symbols are called characters and can be letters, digits, space, punctuation marks and some control characters such as "escape". Each character is represented by a numerical code that is stored as a binary integer.
ASCII	American Standard Code for Information Interchange: a 7-bit character set used by PCs. (There is also an extended ASCII character set that uses 8 bits.)
EBCDIC (pr. eb-sid-ic)	Extended Binary Coded Decimal Interchange Code: an 8-bit character set used by older mainframes.
Unicode	A 16-bit character set that allows many more characters to be coded.

Images

Bitmap image	An image that has been stored as a series of values per pixel. The colour of each individual pixel is stored in a file.
Vector graphic	An image file that is made up of lines and shapes that have certain properties, for example, a line may have the following properties: start-point, end-point, line colour, line thickness, line style. The properties of each shape are stored in a file to make up the image.
Pixel	Short for picture element. It is the smallest component of a bit-mapped image.
Colour depth	The number of bits used to represent the colour of a single pixel in a bitmapped image. Higher colour depth gives a broader range of distinct colours. For example, an image stored as a .gif file uses 8 bits per pixel so the image could use 256 different colours.
Resolution	The number of pixels in an image expressed as: the-number-of-pixels-across x the-number-of-pixels-down eg: 400 x 600.
Metadata	Data about data. In the case of image files metadata is the data the computer needs to interpret the image data in the file, for example: resolution, colour depth and image dimensions.

Sound

Analogue	A continuously changing wave such as natural sound.
Digital	Data that is made up of separate values. How data is stored on a computer.
Sample rate	The number of times per second that the sound wave is measured. The higher the rate the more accurately the sound wave is represented.
Sample interval	The time gap between measurements of the sound wave being taken. Another way of expressing the sampling rate.
Sample resolution	The number of bits used to store the value of each sample. The higher the number of bits the more accurately the value is stored.
ADC	Analogue to Digital converter: takes real-world analogue data and converts it to a binary representation that can be stored on a computer.

Data and Information

Data	Facts and figures with no context or format to give them meaning.
Information	Processed data that has context and format so that it conveys meaning.

Instructions

Instruction set	The group of instructions available for that specific processor to use. The number of instructions available will depend on the number of bits used. For example, with 4 bits there could potentially be 15 different instructions.
Op Code	The group of bits in an instruction that represents the operation such as EAT, MOVE or TURN (See Clarence game p18!)
Compiler	A piece of systems software that converts a program written in a high level programming language into machine code (binary).
Machine Code	A binary representation of a program.
High Level Programming Language	A programming language written in constructs using language we can understand. Languages include Delphi, Visual Basic, Java and C++.

PAST EXAM QUESTIONS & EXAMPLE ANSWERS

From the specimen paper

2 (a) Convert the denary number 106 into an 8 bit binary number.

   128 64 32 16 8 4 2 1   *write in the column headings first*

    0   1   1   0 1 0 1 0   *work out where the 1s go*

   64+32+8+2 = 106   *add them up to check your answer*

   Answer is: 01101010   [2]

   (b) Convert the denary number 106 into Hexadecimal.

   106 / 16 = 6 remainder 10

   10 = A in Hex

   Answer is: 6A   [2]

From Jan 2011 Paper

10 (a) Explain how ASCII is used to represent text in a computer system.

   Each character is given a numeric code ...

   ... that is then stored in binary in the computer.

   ASCII uses 1 byte to store each character.

   The characters coded include letters, digits, punctuation marks ...

   ... and control characters such as tab and enter.   [3]

   (b) State what is meant by the character set of a computer.

   The group of characters that can be represented on that computer   [1]

   (c) Unicode is also used to represent text in a computer system.
       Explain the difference between the character sets of Unicode and ASCII.

   ASCII uses 7 or 8 bits to represent each character so the character set can contain a
   maximum of 256 characters. Unicode uses 16 bits to encode each character so the number of
   characters that can be represented is much higher (65,536 maximum with 16 bits).   [2]

CHAPTER 3:   HARDWARE

In Chapter 1 we looked at the basic components of the computer system. This topic is all about the hardware components in this system and looks at the CPU, Memory, Storage, I/O devices and hardware logic circuits that make up these systems.

THE CENTRAL PROCESSING UNIT (CPU)

The OCR Specification says that you should be able to:

- state the purpose of the CPU
- describe the function of the CPU as fetching and executing instructions stored in memory
- describe cache memory
- explain how common characteristics of CPUs such as clock speed, cache size and number of cores affect their performance

The Central Processing Unit (CPU)

The **central processing unit (CPU)** of a computer is the hardware that executes programs and manages the rest of the hardware. Think of the CPU as the brain of the computer. Just like your brain contains parts that remember things, parts that think and parts that make the rest of your body operate, the CPU does the same for the computer. The CPU is made up of the main memory, the processor and the cache memory (we'll talk about the cache later). The program instructions and data move between the main memory and the processor using internal connections called system buses.

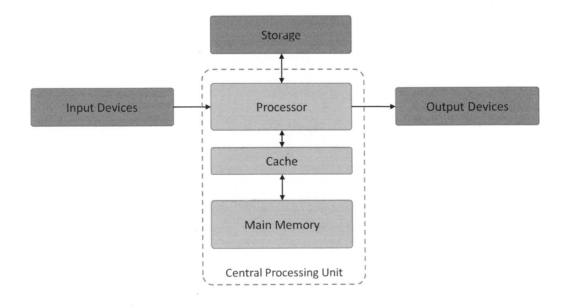

When a program runs on a computer it has to be loaded into the main memory first. From here it can be accessed by the processor to run each instruction in turn. When the program is loaded into main memory the processor is given the start address of where the program is in memory. To run the program the processor fetches an instruction, decodes it and then executes it. The processor executes one instruction at a time. This is called the **fetch-execute cycle**.

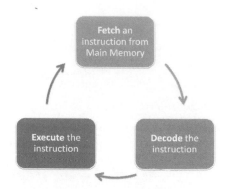

The speed at which a processor operates is quoted as the **clock** speed, in Hertz. Hertz is the name for the number of electrical cycles per second, or the rate at which the electrical current changes in the actual circuits. Everything the processor does happens on the tick of the clock so a faster clock means that more instructions are fetched, decoded and executed in a second. The speed of the processor is measured in MHz (Megahertz) or GHz (Gigahertz). At time of writing (April 2012) processors in a typical home PC's might be rated at 3.2GHz.

CPU Performance

In theory a computer with a 400 MHz processor should operate twice as fast as one with a 200MHz processor but it isn't that simple. There are lots of other components that contribute to the overall speed of the computer. Each one can create a bottleneck in the system and slow it down. Imagine a 3-lane motorway where the traffic can go really fast until it gets to a 1-lane road going into a town. No matter how many lanes you add to the motorway, the 1-lane part of the journey will limit how quickly traffic can get into town. In the same way, a slow component can slow the whole computer down.

??? For you to find out…

Look at some PC adverts in magazines and on the internet to get a feel for current computer specifications.

One bottleneck that can occur is the access speed of main memory. Reading from and writing to main memory is much slower than the speed at which the processor can work. The logical answer is the use faster memory technologies but this increases the price of the computer. Modern computers need to run lots of programs at the same time so they need lots of memory. There needs to be a compromise between speed and cost.

One way of improving speed at minimal cost is to use a small amount of much faster memory where frequently used instructions or data can be stored for a while. We call this special sort of high-speed memory the **cache** (pronounced "cash"). If the processor has to access main memory less often it can work faster so the CPU performance increases.

A typical PC (in April 2012) might have 4, 6 or 8GB of RAM (main memory) but only 2MB of the faster more expensive cache memory. Notice the different units here and remember that there are 1024 Megabytes in a Gigabyte. This computer therefore has 2048 times more RAM than cache!

The purpose of the CPU can be summarised as follows:

- fetch instructions from main memory
- fetch data from main memory
- decode the instructions
- execute the instructions
- performs calculations
- manages the movement of instructions and data to and from peripheral devices

Multi-core Processors

When we looked at the basic fetch-execute cycle we assumed that there was a single processor and a single main memory. You have probably heard terms like "dual-core" and "quad-core" so where do these fit in? Today's more complex CPUs can include more than one processor, or core. A dual-core processor has two processing components within the CPU. A quad core, likewise, has four. In theory having two processors means that the computer can operate twice as fast but this isn't always the case.

Imagine a bakery where one chef is making cakes. If you brought in three more chefs they could all make their own cakes and the bakery would make four times as many cakes. If there was only one recipe though you couldn't have cook 1 doing the first line of the recipe, cook 2 doing line 2, cook 3 doing line 3 and so on. Cook 2 would need to wait for the first cook to mix the flour and butter before he could fold in the eggs! So four cooks working their way through one recipe wouldn't be any quicker, in fact it is just more complicated (you've heard the saying "Too many cooks...."!). Likewise a program is a series of instructions that need to be done in order. Multiple processors could work on different programs that operate in parallel but unless the computer is designed to use multiple cores it isn't necessarily four times faster. On the whole though, a PC with lots of programs going on at the same time will have a multiple-core processor and will operate quicker than a single-core processor.

MEMORY

The OCR Specification says that you should be able to:

- describe the difference between RAM and ROM
- explain the need for ROM in a computer system
- describe the purpose of RAM in a computer system
- explain how the amount of RAM in a personal computer affects the performance of the computer
- explain the need for virtual memory
- discuss how changes in memory technologies are leading to innovative computer designs

Memory in a computer system refers to the components that store (or remember!) things. There are different types of memory with different purposes. Some are very fast and expensive such as the cache memory discussed earlier, and some are cheaper and slower such as the memory sticks you probably use at school.

These different types of memory have different characteristics and can be compared in terms of their access speed (how quickly you can read from them or write to them), their price and the whether they can store data when the power is turned off (volatility). Let's consider some common types of memory in computer systems:

Random Access Memory (RAM)

RAM is the type of memory used in the computer's main memory. Many people say "RAM" when they mean main memory. Nothing in a computer is really "random" so random access just refers to the fact that you can write anywhere in that memory space at any time, you don't have to put the next thing straight after the last one like you do on a magnetic tape, for example.

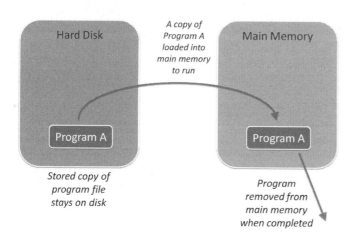

As we said earlier in the chapter, when a program is running it has to be loaded from the hard disk into the main memory so the processor can access the instructions. Any data needed for that program to run is also loaded into main memory while the program is running. The main purpose of RAM is to act as temporary storage for programs and data, just for the duration of that program. Once the program has finished and is closed, it is no longer in main memory.

So why doesn't the processor get the instructions straight from the disk? It is about access speed. Reading from and writing to a hard disk is very slow compared to the speed of the processor. Just as we used the high speed cache between the processor and main memory we need main memory to store the programs currently in use or the computer would be really slow.

As every program in use should, ideally, be in main memory while it runs, the amount of main memory also affects the performance of the computer. If a computer system has lots of programs running at the same time it needs lots of main memory.

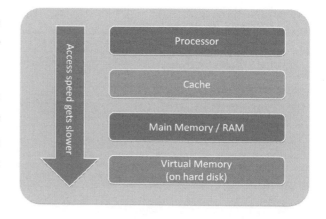

Virtual Memory

Sometimes there just isn't enough main memory for all the programs that need to run. Computers can be configured so part of the hard disk behaves like main memory. This is called **virtual memory**. The access speed on a hard disk is much slower than the speed of RAM so this isn't ideal. It is used to store parts of programs currently being run but the parts actually being executed still need to be in main memory. As the processor gets to the next part of the program, sections are swapped between virtual memory and main memory. Sometimes this works well but sometimes the computer spends more fetch-execute cycles swapping bits around than it does executing the program!

Volatility

When you are in the middle of a piece of work at school and your "friend" turns the computer off you will notice that you lose the work you did since you last saved! This is because the saved version goes onto the hard disk but the most recent version was only in main memory/RAM when the power went off. RAM is described as **volatile**, it loses its contents if there is no power. The hard disk is designed for long term storage of files and is **non-volatile** memory.

Read Only Memory (ROM)

RAM is volatile so when you turn off your computer it loses its contents. When you turn the computer back on it needs to get the basic startup routine from somewhere that is not volatile! The operating system and all you programs will be stored on the hard disk but these need to be loaded into RAM to run.

The computer has a piece of software called the **bootstrap loader**. This is a small program that loads the operating system. Once the operating system is loaded it takes care of the rest. The term comes from the idea that when you're not doing very well in life you can "pull yourself up by your bootstraps"! In this day and age you're more likely to hear "sort yourself out" but the meaning is the same - you are in effect getting yourself restarted. Bootstrapping became abbreviated to booting, a term you have probably heard before. To "boot" a computer is to start it up from scratch.

ROM is Read Only Memory; you cannot write over the contents once it has been created. It is also non-volatile; you can leave the computer switched off for months and it will still start up as soon as it has power again. RAM on the other hand is only used for temporary storage of programs when they are running. RAM is read-write and volatile.

ROM	RAM
Read only	Read – write
Not volatile	Volatile

Secondary Memory

Main memory is also known as **Primary Memory** or **Immediate Access Store**. Memory is all about storage so, strictly speaking, storage devices such as hard disks are also a type of memory. These long-term, non-volatile types of storage are also called **Secondary Memory**.

Typically a PC will have a hard disk that stores all the files long term but secondary memory/storage also includes memory sticks, floppy disks (seldom used these days), tapes and CDs. These are discussed further in the next section, "Secondary Storage".

SECONDARY STORAGE

The OCR Specification says that you should be able to:

- explain the need for secondary storage
- describe common storage technologies such as optical, magnetic and solid state
- describe flash memory
- select suitable storage devices and storage media for a given application and justify their choice using characteristics such as capacity, speed, portability, durability and reliability

We all want to store files over a long period of time. We keep photographs, projects, music, films, letters and spreadsheets on our computers. We also expect our programs to be there when we switch the computer on. This long term storage is sometimes called **Secondary Memory** or **Secondary Storage** (primary memory is the main memory).

Secondary storage is usually much larger and, as we want such a lot of it, it needs to be cheap. Cheaper memory technologies tend to have slower access speeds than main memory, as discussed earlier. Secondary memory is non-volatile and needs to be robust and reliable. Has your memory stick been through the washing machine yet?!

Choosing the right type of storage medium for a particular use is important. You need to consider the following features:

- **Capacity**: How much space there is to store files. Compare the size of a floppy disk at 1.44MB to a CD that can store 700MB. You can only fit half of this book on a floppy disk.
- **Speed**: How quickly the computer can read data from a storage device or write data to it. When you write to an external hard disk or memory stick make sure you wait for the light to go out before you unplug it!
- **Portability**: Can you easily unplug it and carry it away? Does it fit in a pencil case or do you need a large bag!
- **Durability**: How easily is it damaged? Will it survive dropping or having coffee tipped on it?
- **Reliability**: How long will it last? Anything with moving parts is likely to be less reliable.

There are different storage technologies available:

- Magnetic:

This is the oldest of the technologies and is used in floppy disks, hard disks and tapes. It is cheap and high capacity (stores a lot of data). Magnetic disks are read with a moving head inside the disk drive and magnetic tapes are read by moving the tape past a read-write head. Moving parts make these media quite slow to read from or write to and moving parts go wrong more often than solid state media. Magnetic media are also vulnerable to damage as well. Just as a video tape left on a stereo speaker is damaged by the magnets, so too a magnetic disk or tape can be easily wiped.

MAGNETIC STORAGE DEVICES		
	Internal Hard Disk	**Portable Hard Disk**	**Magnetic Tape**
Cost	Very cheap but not as cheap as tape 1TB internal for £90		Cheapest bulk data storage medium 72GB tape £10
Capacity	Up to 1TB		
Access Speed	3Gb/s	480Mb/s *(speed of USB2 interface)*	Slow access speed because tape drive has to read through the tape serially.
Portability	Not portable, built in to PC	Can fit in a large pocket	Cassette tape is compact but needs a tape drive to use.
Durability	Good durability when disk not in use but vulnerable to movement when spinning. Can write to the disk an infinite number of times. Affected by heat and magnetic fields.		Limited lifetime - wears out with repeated use. If used once for archiving can last 15 years. Affected by heat and magnetic fields.
Reliability	Extremely reliable		Very reliable if not damaged
Typical use	Inside a PC as secondary storage	Supplementary storage for a PC or portable storage where high capacity is required	Good for backups and archiving but access speed is too slow for general use.

Internal hard drive (opened)

External hard drive

- Optical Storage media:

The word "optical" should make you think about the eye and how we see the world in terms of reflected light. Optical media work in a similar way. Lasers write data to the disc and read data from it. Optical media include CDs and DVDs.

MAGNETIC STORAGE DEVICES		
	CD	DVD
Cost	Very cheap 50 CD-R for £12 (24p each)	Very cheap 50 x 4.7GB DVD-R for £15 (30p each)
Capacity	640 MB	4-17 GB
Access Speed	Up to 7.6 MB/s (52x)	16 MB/s (12x)
	Much slower than magnetic hard disk	
Portability	Easy to carry in a large pocket or bag	Easy to carry in a large pocket or bag
Durability	Depends on how it is stored Quality degrades over time, life expectancy of a CD-R about 20 to 100 years but can start degrading in 18 months!	Recordings last 2-15 years so not considered reliable for long term storage.
Reliability	Good for medium term but degrades over time	
Typical use	CD-ROM for software distribution CD-R or CD-RW for backup/archive	Backup/archive where higher capacity is needed

- Solid State/Flash Storage media:

If you need to move work from school to your home PC you might use a USB Memory Stick (sometimes called a pen drive). These use a newer technology called **Flash memory**. It is **solid-state** memory, which just means that it does not have any moving parts. This makes the access speed of flash memory very high (but not as fast as RAM) and there is less to go wrong. Flash memory is a type of RAM but will not replace the type of RAM used in the main memory as its access speed is too slow. It is however, an excellent replacement for a hard disk in devices like notebooks and tablet PCs. This type of memory is also used in mobile phones, tablet PCs and cameras.

??? For you to find out...

How much storage/memory there is on a modern camera?

How do hard disks and CD ROMs work?

	FLASH STORAGE DEVICES		
	Internal Solid State/Flash Storage	USB Memory Stick	Memory Card
Cost	128GB for £120	32GB for £45 64GB for £120	32GB SD card £25
Capacity	256 GB	64MB to 64 GB	128 MB to 4 GB
Access Speed	6Gb/s *(faster than magnetic disk because no moving parts)*	480Mb/s *(speed of USB2 interface)*	*Dependent on type of card and device interface*
Portability	Not portable, built into PC	Very small, can put in any pocket or on a key-ring	Very small, designed for portable devices
Durability	More robust than hard disks with moving parts. Said to be 5-10 times more durable than a hard disk drive	Very durable – often survive washing machine! Some can be snapped quite easily.	Very durable - not sensitive to temperature or knocks.
Reliability	Extremely reliable	Very reliable but can corrupt files if removed from PC too soon	Very reliable
Typical use	Notebooks, tablets, slim laptops	Personal use, moving files between computers	In phones and cameras

Storage Media Capacity Compared

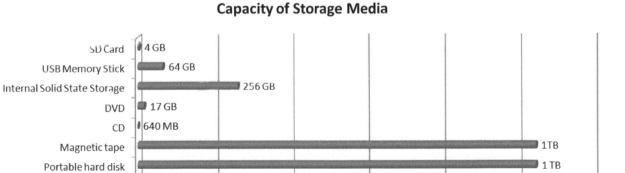

Capacity of Storage Media

- SD Card — 4 GB
- USB Memory Stick — 64 GB
- Internal Solid State Storage — 256 GB
- DVD — 17 GB
- CD — 640 MB
- Magnetic tape — 1 TB
- Portable hard disk — 1 TB
- Internal Hard Disk — 1 TB

!!! **Please note...**

Details in the above tables and graph may already be out of date (written Feb 2012).

You should research products that are currently on the market to see how quickly technology advances.

INNOVATIVE COMPUTER DESIGN

The OCR Specification says that you should be able to:

- discuss how changes in memory technologies are leading to innovative computer designs

Computer technology changes very quickly so you should keep in touch with current changes by reading magazines and websites that are up to date. Memory technologies are changing in several ways so consider how these factors affect the products coming into shops now. These factors include:

- **Capacity and density:** You can now buy a 64GB SD card for a camera where a couple of years ago an 4GB card was considered high capacity. Increasing capacity isn't too challenging, just add more cards. The ability to increase the capacity on the same size card is the challenge. Higher density means devices can store more without getting bigger, or devices can store the same amount but get smaller. You only have to look at mobile phones to see how these have become smaller and lighter and yet can still now store more music and even video. The capacity of primary memory has also improved so computers can run more applications at the same time and complex games can run easily on today's "basic" computers.

- **Speed:** Although Flash memory is still much slower than RAM it is significantly faster than a magnetic hard disk. This means that bulky and sensitive hard disks can be replaced with smaller, lighter, faster and more reliable flash memory. Computers start up quicker as this is dependent on how long it takes to load the operating system from secondary storage into RAM. So now we have notebooks you can slip into a pocket, tablet PCs and smart-phones that behave like computers.

- **Price:** Flash memory is cheaper and easier to produce so devices using flash memory become cheaper as well. Lower cost memory has improved the capacity of gadgets like MP3 players, hand-held game consoles and phones. The cost of RAM has dropped so a £500 PC today has more RAM and more storage than a £500 PC just a couple of years ago.

INPUT & OUTPUT DEVICES

The OCR Specification says that you should be able to:

- understand the need for input and output devices
- describe suitable input devices for a wide range of computer controlled situations
- describe suitable output devices for a wide range of computer controlled situations
- discuss input and output devices for users with specific needs

This book does not attempt to describe the full range of devices currently available. There are many websites that comprehensively describe how these work. It is however important to understand what input and output devices exist and how to choose appropriate devices for a situation.

Input Devices

We live in an analogue world of continuously changing variables. In order to process or store data we must somehow capture it and convert it into a digital representation. Chapter 2, "Data Representation", describes how we store text, numbers, sound, images and instructions on a computer. Here we are concerned with the devices that will capture the inputs.

Keyboard: Used for data entry into computers. This is a full keyboard with functions keys and a number pad but laptops and other devices may have cut-down versions of this. Pressing a key generates a character code into the computer.

Mouse: Used to point at objects on the screen and select items by clicking or double-clicking. Right-click usually generates a context-sensitive menu. A scroll wheel between the buttons makes it easy to move up and down the screen. Attached to the computer by a wire and USB connector or wirelessly. The mouse detects movements and position either with a ball or a reflected light source under the mouse. A variation on the mouse is a **trackerball** where the user moves a larger ball on the top surface instead.

Touch screen: Used on phones and tablet PCs as well as applications such as help screens in banks and tourist information offices. Instead of using a mouse you can just touch the icons to select them. On some devices moving two fingers apart of together on the screen zooms in or out and tapping icons is equivalent to a double-click.

Barcode scanner: A laser scans the barcode on a product to detect the width of the black and white stripes. This generates the product number so the rest of the details can be found in a database.

OMR: Optical Mark Recognition is used for things like multiple choice tests, evaluation forms and lottery tickets. This uses a light source that reflects a different amount of light back from shaded boxes to detect the data for input.

OCR: Similar to OMR but this is Optical Character Recognition. The software interprets the marks as characters and generates text and some formatting detail into a word processing file.

Joystick: Although you probably think of a game controller, joysticks do have other uses! They are used to control wheelchairs and to remotely control lights, security cameras and bomb disposal robots. The game controller's cross-shaped control pad is a joystick, just flattened!

Microphone: used to input sound that can either be recorded in a file or processed by voice recognition software for other uses. Voice recognition could be used for many applications such as hands-free phone dialing, controlling devices in a house if you are not mobile, a karaoke game or for security identification.

Sensors: These measure temperature, light levels, pressure, humidity and many other analogue events in the real world. These can then trigger processes and the appropriate output action as required. For example, if a thermistor (temperature sensor) reading is higher than 23°C, the computer could signal motors to open the greenhouse windows (see "actuators" in output devices). The sensor shown is an Xbox movement sensor.

Sensors are also used to track eye movement or head movement to allow disabled people to use computers. Eye and head movements operate a pointer on the screen, instead of using a mouse.

Specialised keyboards: There are many variations on the keyboard and touch-screen that allow people with various disabilities to operate a computer. Features may include: bigger keys, specialised layouts for different purposes, braille overlays and brighter colours for contrast.

Foot-operated mouse: This works in the same way as a normal mouse, complete with left and right-click buttons. It is designed to be easily operated with a foot instead.

Camera: A camera can be used as a web-cam so you can see the person you are phoning over the internet but it can also be a way of communicating with the computer if you do not have the use of your hands. Instead of using a mouse a disabled person can control an on-screen keyboard with eye or head movements detected with a camera

Sip-and-Puff Switches: These are activated by the user's breath. A "puff" into the device might be the equivalent of a mouse click and a "sip" (or suck) might be the equivalent of holding a key down. This would be used with an on-screen keyboard.

??? **For you to find out...**

Use www.howstuffworks.com to find out how these devices work.

Output Devices

Computer systems create many outputs for us. These can be printed reports, data on a screen, sound, pictures or an action that needs performing via a motorised control. Here are some output devices you may come across:

CRT Monitor: CRT stands for Cathode Ray Tube. These are the old fashioned monitors that are really deep on the desk and weigh a ton! Very few people use these now because they are heavy and take up too much space but in places like factories they are still used because the glass screen is more robust than the TFT screen.

TFT Monitor: TFT stands for Thin Film Transistor. This type of screen is the thin screen you probably have at home or on a laptop. This is a variation on LCD technology. LCD stands for Liquid Crystal Display, the earlier version of TFT screens. These screen take up less space but are more easily damaged than a CRT monitor.

Speakers: To output sound the computer must synthesise sound from the digital file and output sound waves through speakers. These might be small speakers integrated into the computer, phone or other device, or they may be stand-alone speakers that attach to the computer by a headphone jack, for example.

Headphones: Personal speakers!

Inkjet printer: Probably the type of printer you have at home. It works by spraying ink onto the page so if you have big shaded areas on a page the page will come out a bit damp and wrinkled! For normal text they produce good quality printing at a low cost. The ink is never sealed on the page so if you use a highlighter pen on notes from an inkjet the ink will smudge. They are also quite slow so they are not suitable for a large office or classroom.

Laser printer: This is the type of printer you probably have in the classroom as it is quicker and quieter than an inkjet. The ink is in the form of a toner power that is sealed onto the page by heated rollers. That is why your printing comes out warm. The ink goes on to the page dry so the quality is much better and it won't smudge. These are more expensive printers and the toner cartridges are more expensive than inkjet cartridges.

Dot-matrix printer: Before inkjet and laser printers we had dot-matrix printers. They worked a bit like a typewriter as a print head has to strike the paper through an ink ribbon to print text on a page. It is called an impact printer for this reason. They are still used today where companies have to use multi-part stationery. A laser printer would only print on the top page but an impact printer pushes through several layers that have carbon paper on the back. The paper is fed through the printer using the holes at the side. The holes are then torn off to give a printed page.

Braille Printer: An impact printer that creates raised dots to represent each letter to allow blind people to read

Actuator: The actuator is the device that performs some sort of mechanical action based on inputs. For example, a voice sensor might trigger a motor to close the curtains. Often these are used with sensors but can also be used with touch screens. Modern aeroplanes use many sensors to provide inputs to computers that control the flight. Actuators move the flaps on the wings and the tail automatically.

Lights (LEDs): Lights are used to show that Caps Lock is on or that the computer is in standby or that the laptop is connected to the mains. Light Emitting Diodes (LEDs) are used to output lots of signals to the user.

Appropriate I/O devices

In an exam you may be asked to identify suitable input and output (often abbreviated to i/o) devices for certain situations. We are all very familiar with a standard PC but think about how computers are used in different situations.

Supermarket Point of Sale (POS): The checkout at a supermarket has a wide range of input devices. The barcode scanner will get a product number from the purchase, which will then enable the checkout to get all the details from a database somewhere else in the store. The checkout has a weight sensor/scales for fruit and vegetables as well. The checkout operator must be able to type in product numbers when they don't scan and will also have a touch-screen to quickly find produce such as apples that are being weighed. When the customer pays, the checkout will need to read credit card details and the checkout operator might swipe a loyalty card. Credit cards will have the card number stored on a chip but loyalty cards generally just have a magnetic stripe to store the customer ID.

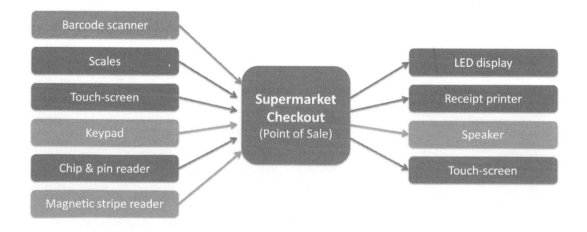

Automated house for a disabled person: If you are in a wheelchair or find it hard to move around your home then simple tasks like closing the curtains or answering the door can be very difficult. Computers can be used to make these tasks easier to do so people can live in their own homes still. Input devices can be a variety of sensors that trigger actions. For example, movement sensors that trigger lights and pressure sensors that open doors. A digital camera and a microphone at the front door can link to a monitor, speakers and microphone in the house so the person doesn't have to go to the door just to tell a doorstep salesperson to go away! A touch screen can be used to control curtains, lights, heating, television and radio.

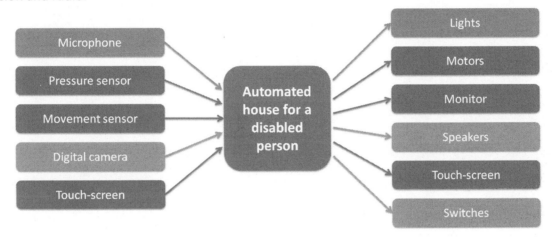

Patient monitoring in a hospital: Patients in a critical condition are linked up to computers that monitor their blood pressure, temperature, breathing rate and depth. These all use sensors of some kind. The output that nurses check will be on a monitor showing the current readings but also there will be speakers that produce alarms if readings drop below certain limits and also printers that produce a history of readings. To set the machine up the nurse will probably have a touch-screen and there may be some settings displayed in LEDs.

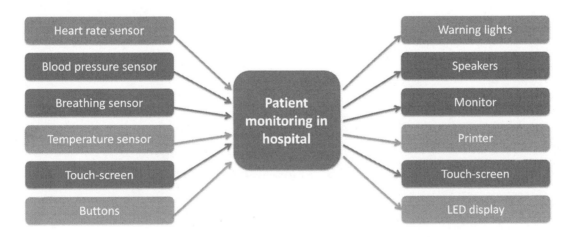

These are just a few ideas, you need to research and consider other scenarios and consider the appropriate I/O devices to use.

BINARY LOGIC

The OCR Specification says that you should be able to:

- explain why data is represented in computer systems in binary form
- understand and produce simple logic diagrams using the operations NOT, AND and OR
- produce a truth table from a given logic diagram

Binary Logic in Programming

Understanding how binary logic works will also help your programming. In your programs you often use complex boolean expressions to control loops and selection statements, for example:

```
While NOT(EndOfFile) AND NOT (ItemFound)......

IF (X<=10) OR (CurrentCharNum>LengthOfString) THEN ......
```

You have probably programmed a repeat loop to carry on until the user typed a "Y" or a "y". The loop would look something like this with the condition at the end:

```
Repeat
    |
    |
Until (response = 'Y') or (response = 'y')
```

          A Boolean   **Another Boolean**
          Expression   **Expression!**

*A condition in programming is made up of **Boolean Expressions** that are either true or false*

Each **Boolean expression** can be replaced with a letter, this is called a **Boolean variable**.

```
Until (response = 'Y') or (response = 'y')
```

        Replace with the Boolean   **Replace with the Boolean**
           variable, X   **variable, Y**

```
Until        X        or        Y
```

Just like the Boolean data type in programming, Boolean variables are either true or false. X and Y will be either true or false. We represent true with 1 and false with 0 to represent electronic circuits being open or closed, just we did with binary!

Circuit closed = 1 = True   Circuit open = 0 = False

Truth Tables

If you have more than one Boolean expression in a condition then you can use **Truth Tables** to show the outcomes.

Q = X AND Y

X	Y	Q
0	0	0
0	1	0
1	0	0
1	1	1

For (X AND Y) to be true, X must be true and Y must be true so all three of these combinations are false.

(X AND Y) is true because X is true and Y is true

Q = X OR Y

X	Y	Q
0	0	0
0	1	1
1	0	1
1	1	1

X is false and so is Y so (X OR Y) is false

Although X is false, Y is true so (X OR Y) is true

Although Y is false, X is true so (X OR Y) is true

(X OR Y) is true if either X or Y is true, here they are both true

Q = NOT X

X	Q
0	1
1	0

NOT X is the opposite of X so 0 becomes 1 in this case

NOT X is the opposite of X so 1 becomes 0 in this case

These basic gates can be combined into more complex expressions, for example:

Q = NOT (X AND Y)

X	Y	X AND Y	Q
0	0	0	1
0	1	0	1
1	0	0	1
1	1	1	0

Logic Diagrams

As we saw in Chapter 2, "Data Representation", computers are based on electrical circuits where we can detect whether current is flowing or not. Binary is base 2, where we have just two possible values, 1 or 0, so representing data as binary values means we just have to detect these two values in electrical circuits.

Binary logic is about these most basic circuits. Circuits in computers are made up of many logic gates but at this level we are just looking at three basic logic gates: AND, OR and NOT. With two inputs to each of these we can generate an output based on the logic gate in use.

We use specific symbols to represent the different logic gates, these are standard symbols. They can be used to represent boolean expressions such as Q = NOT A AND (B OR C).

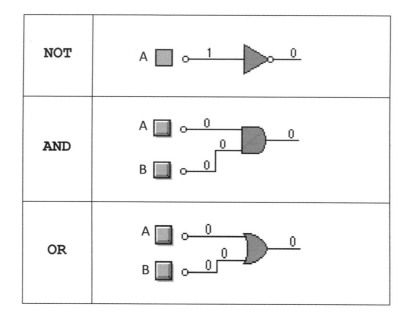

The logics gates can be joined up to make a circuit. For example:

NOT (A OR (B AND C))

GLOSSARY OF TERMS

CPU

CPU	The central processing unit that contains the processor, main memory and cache.
Main memory/RAM	Also known as Immediate Access Store and Primary Memory The memory in the CPU that is used to temporarily store programs while they are running and data used by these programs. The processor fetches instructions from main memory. Memory is made up of many addressable locations.
Processor	The component in the computer that fetches, decodes and executes instructions.
Cache	High speed memory in the CPU that is used to store a copy of frequently used instructions and data. Faster access speed than main memory. Used to improve CPU performance.
Clock speed	Measured in hertz or cycles per second, the clock speed represents how many instructions per second the processor can execute. The higher the clock speed the faster the CPU can operate.
System Buses	The circuits/internal wiring that connect the processor and main memory together.
Fetch Execute Cycle	The process by which a program is run: instructions are stored in main memory, fetched by the processor one at a time, decoded and executed.
Dual-Core / Quad-Core	A CPU that contains multiple processor components (cores) that can operate independently to process more than one task at a time.

Memory

RAM	Random Access Memory: a type of memory that is read-write and volatile. Used for Main Memory.
ROM	Read Only Memory: memory that is hard-coded at the time of manufacture. Stores the start up programs, the boot-strap loader.
Bootstrap Loader	The first program that is loaded into main memory from ROM when a computer is switched on. This will load the operating system from secondary storage.

Memory (continued)

Volatile	Describes memory that loses its contents when the power is turned off. Eg: main memory
Non-Volatile	Describes memory that does not lose its contents when the power is turned off. Eg: hard disk.
Secondary Memory	Long term, non-volatile storage media such as hard disks, memory sticks, magnetic tapes & CDs.
Virtual Memory	Part of the hard disk that is configured to behave as an extension to main memory.
Magnetic Media	Secondary storage such as hard disks, tape and floppy disks.
Optical Media	Secondary storage that is read using lasers such as CDs and DVDs.
Solid State / Flash Memory	Secondary storage that has no moving parts. Used in memory sticks, cameras and phones.
Pen Drive	Another term for a USB memory stick

Binary Logic

Boolean Expression	An expression that is either true or false eg: X=10
Truth Table	A table that shows all the possible combinations of inputs and their logical output value.
Logical Operators	AND, OR, NOT
Logic Diagram	A diagram of a circuit showing logic gates with inputs and the output these generate.

From the specimen paper

2 Mary's computer has an 800MHz CPU and 1GB of RAM.

(a) Describe the purpose of the CPU.

The CPU controls the operations of the computer.

It fetches, decodes and executes instructions.   [2]

(b) Mary wants to upgrade this computer so that she can play the latest games.

Explain two ways by which the computer can be upgraded to improve its performance.

Replace the processor with a higher speed processor: higher speed will increase the number of instructions that can be executed per second.

Add more main memory/RAM: more main memory means it can hold more programs at any one time so the computer will have to use the slower virtual memory less.   [4]

(c) A computer shop tells Mary that she would be better off buying a new computer, than upgrading the computer that she already has. However, Mary wants to consider the environmental impact as well as the cost.

Discuss the advantages and disadvantages of buying a new computer instead of upgrading and advise Mary on what she should do. You should focus on the environmental impact and the cost.

[Quality of written communication will be assessed on this question]

In terms of cost, Mary should consider that technology is getting cheaper so she will be able to buy a much higher performance machine for similar money to the old one. Also, buying individual components can work out quite expensive, especially if she has to pay someone else to fit them for her. With technology moving on so quickly, there may also be issues with actually buying compatible components.

Mary would need to offset the advantages of buying a new computer against the environmental cost of manufacturing as well as the issues involved with disposing of some parts of the old computer. A newer computer may be more power-efficient than the old one but a higher performance machine may use more power.

If the upgrade can be done cheaply I would advise her to do that. If not she could replace the computer but find an alternative use for the old one - perhaps someone who doesn't need such high performance could use it.   [6]

10 The following logic circuit can be written as P = NOT (A AND B)

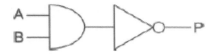

(a)   State the output(P) of the circuit if the inputs are:

(i)   A = 1   B = 0

P =   *1*   [1]

(ii)   A = 1   B = 1

P =   *0*   [1]

(b)   Draw the logic circuit for P = (A OR B) AND C

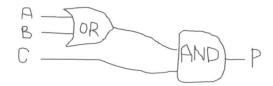

[2]

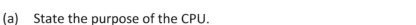

From Jan 2011 Paper

1   Jo buys a notebook computer which has a 3MHz quad-core central processing unit (CPU).

(a)   State the purpose of the CPU.

The CPU controls the operations of the computer.

It fetches, decodes and executes instructions.   [1]

(b)   Describe what is meant by:

3MHz CPU

3 MHz is the clock speed, how fast the processor works.
Hertz is clock cycles per second and indicates how many instructions per second
the processor can execute.   [2]

quad-core CPU

The CPU contains 4 processor components, each working independently so the
CPU can process more than one task at a time.   [2]

4   A desk-top computer's memory includes ROM and RAM.

Tick **one** box in each row to show whether each of the statements is true for ROM or RAM.

	ROM	RAM
Programs and data which are currently in use are loaded here.		✓
All the contents are lost when the power is turned off.		✓
It is used to boot up the computer when it is switched on.	✓	

[3]

CHAPTER 4: SOFTWARE

Software is any program that runs on the computer. There are many different types of software including operating systems, games, word processing packages, virus checkers, spreadsheets, programming language translators (see Chapter 7, "Programming") and many more. These are grouped into different categories. The two main categories are:

- **System software:**

  Programs that are used to run the computer, including the operating system, utilities, library routines and programming language translators.

- **Applications:**

  Programs that perform a task for a user. This is something that the user would do with or without a computer, it the task that matters not the computer.

To see the difference think, "Would I need this software if I didn't have a computer?". For example, you would use a word processing package to write a letter but the task could still be done another way. The letter still needs writing. On the other hand, a virus checker only exists because of the computer, it isn't a task the user would otherwise do.

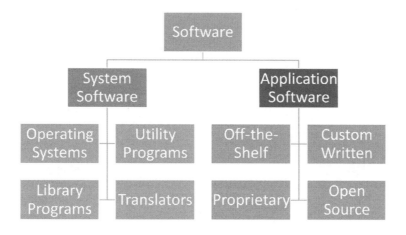

System software includes **operating systems** and **utilities**, both of which we look at in more detail later in this chapter. This category also includes the **translators** that convert the programs you write into machine code; each programming language has a compiler or interpreter. **Library programs** are modules of code that can be used in your programs. For example, if you write a program to work in Windows you can build in standard functionality such as the Open File dialogue box rather than writing it yourself. In Delphi programs, statements like "Uses StringUtils" will import procedures that have already been written for you, in this case all the string handling functions. These are all library modules.

Application Software can be categorised in different ways. For GCSE Computing we will consider the different ways in which it can be sourced.

OPERATING SYSTEMS

The OCR Specification says that you should be able to:

- explain the need for the following functions of an operating system: user interface, memory management, peripheral management, multi-tasking and security

The operating system is system software. It is a group of programs that manages the computer's resources. This includes the following functions:

- Memory management
- Peripheral management
- Multi-tasking
- Security
- Providing a user interface

Memory Management

When a program is running it must be in the computer's main memory. The main memory has a finite size. The operating system must manage where in memory the programs will go.

When you start up a program on the computer, the operating system copies it from the disk into main memory and gives the processor the **address** (location) of where it starts. The processor can then fetch, decode and execute each instruction in turn.

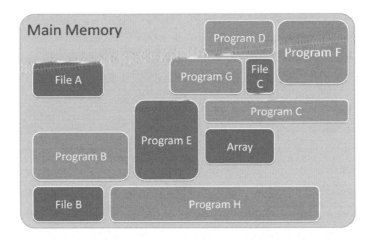

As the program runs it will also use data. In modern computers the programs and the data they use are stored in the same main memory. When a program runs, the variable declarations at the start will set up locations in memory, allocating appropriate space, based on the data types. For example, a variable that has the data type "integer" takes up two bytes in memory, whereas a string variable may be allocated 255 bytes. The memory management part of the operating system will need to manage space used by the programs in this way.

```
var
    count:integer;
    average:real;
    testScores: array [1..10] of integer;
```

} Variables that will be set up in memory before the program starts

If a data file is accessed, data from that too must be brought into main memory. The operating system tracks where programs and data are stored using **addresses**. Each location in memory has a unique numerical address. (In assembly language you use these and normally refer to them in hex because human being as are not very good with long sequences of binary!).

The operating system tracks where programs and data are at any time to make efficient use of the space in memory and to make sure nothing gets overwritten by something else. As a program is finished it can be removed from memory and as new ones are run they will be loaded into memory.

Multi-tasking / Process Management

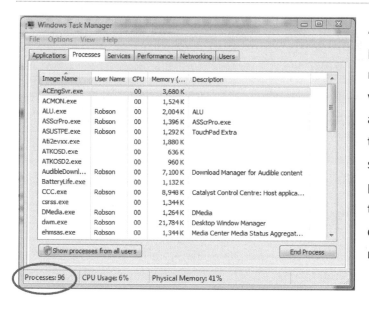

A modern computer is running many programs at once, it is **multi-tasking**. A user may have several documents open as well as various websites. The operating system will also be running lots of background tasks just to manage the computer itself. The screen shot to the left shows that there were 96 processes running on my laptop while I was typing this paragraph! (A **process** is what we call a program when it is running in main memory).

A processor can only execute one instruction at a time (assumes single core processor). The processes are taking it in turns using the processor to execute instructions but because it happens so quickly it looks like they are all happening at the same time. The operating system has to manage all of these programs to make sure each one gets enough processor time. Some programs are clearly more urgent or important than others so there are priorities to manage as well. A program that deals with a hardware error will take priority over a word processing package trying to make text bold! While one program is being executed by the processor, other programs wait in main memory.

!!! **For you to do...**

Type Ctrl+Alt+Del to look at Task Manager on your computer and see how many processes are running.

Peripheral Management

Peripherals are any computer hardware components that are not part of the CPU. This includes input devices, output devices and storage. For some of these the term peripheral makes sense; the keyboard and monitor are outside the main computer casing but storage is not as obvious. Although a hard disk is usually inside the computer casing, it is still considered a peripheral as it is outside the CPU (processor & main memory). Portable hard disks, memory sticks and CDs are also storage devices but these are more obviously peripheral to the main system as they are outside of the computer casing.

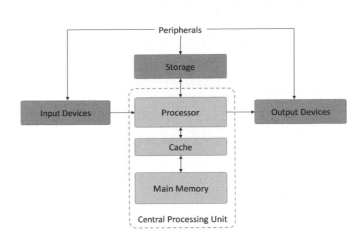

A function of the operating system is to manage these devices. In Chapter 3, "Hardware", we looked at the different speeds of components. Writing to storage or an output device is much slower than moving data around in the CPU. The operating system will use buffers (queues) to make sure that data is not lost. Reading from storage and getting data from input devices is also slow. When the processor needs input from a user (waiting for them to click "OK" perhaps), the operating system may allow other programs to use the processor. Imagine how you use your own computer. You might be typing an essay while listening to music, while downloading an album from the internet and real-time messaging a friend. All of this at the same time! The operating system manages all of this.

Security

Your phone, laptop, tablet or PC can all have passwords set to make them more secure. These can be set for different users on a PC but on a personal device like a phone the password is likely to be for the

device. You can also password protect individual files on the computer or set certain files as read-only for some users so they can view them but they cannot change them.

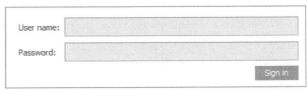

The type of security offered by the operating system will depend on the type of computer system. The operating system on a PC is very complex and has different types and levels of security to offer. The computer in a washing machine just has to make sure the "user" isn't allowed to open the door when the machine is full of water. You don't see many washing machines with passwords!

The operating system is the software that manages this security. The operating system software on a PC may include additional features, or utilities, that make the computer easier to maintain and use. These include virus checking software, a firewall and parental controls.

Providing a User Interface

The user interface is the way in which we interact with computer hardware. We are all familiar with the way a PC works: click icons with the mouse, scrolling up and down pages, typing into forms etc. This is called a WIMP user interface. WIMP stands for Windows, Icons, Menus and Pointers.

Mobile phones and tablet PCs have a slightly different user interface that allows you to move things with your fingers and can sense when you tip the device. Phones have buttons down the side that perform specific functions such as recording sound or turning on a camera.

Some computer systems are embedded into everyday machines such as cars and central heating controls. Users interact with these in very different ways. The operating systems have to provide appropriate ways for the user to interact with these as well.

Some computers have a **command-line interface**; no mouse or menus just a text prompt where the user types a command. On a PC we sometimes need a simple and direct interface with the hardware so within MS Windows we can use the Command Prompt, which is an example of a command line interface.

```
Command Prompt

c:\Susan's Stuff>cd computing

c:\Susan's Stuff\Computing>dir
 Volume in drive C is VistaOS
 Volume Serial Number is 94A1-B9F4

 Directory of c:\Susan's Stuff\Computing

25/08/2011  07:55    <DIR>          .
25/08/2011  07:55    <DIR>          ..
09/11/2008  20:34    <DIR>          Boolean Algebra
05/07/2007  13:57               543 csunplugged AI activity.htm
25/08/2011  07:55    <DIR>          csunplugged AI activity_files
02/11/2008  16:23            66,913 DRM diagram.gif
11/11/2008  10:54               394 FirstWebPage.html
11/11/2008  10:54    <DIR>          Web SIte Design
               3 File(s)         67,850 bytes
               5 Dir(s)   9,203,466,240 bytes free

c:\Susan's Stuff\Computing>
```

Whatever method is used for the user to communicate with a computer or computerised device, it is the operating system that provides these features.

Utility Programs

> The OCR Specification says that you should be able to:
>
> - describe the purpose and use of common utility programs for computer security (antivirus, spyware protection and firewalls), disk organisation (formatting, file transfer, and defragmentation), and system maintenance (system information and diagnosis, system cleanup tools, automatic updating)

Strictly speaking the operating system is the software that controls and manages the computer system but most operating systems also include programs called **utilities**. Utilities are not essential for the computer to work but either make it easy for the user to use it in some way or provide housekeeping functionality. We can categorise these utilities as follows:

- Security utilities that keep your computer safe from hackers and viruses.

- Disk organisation utilities that organise your files into folders and tidy up the disk.

- Maintenance utilities that perform system diagnostics and get software updates.

Security Utilities

Security is about keeping the computer system safe from hazards. Hazards come in many forms but includes viruses, hackers and spyware. To keep this in perspective though, the most dangerous thing a computer has to face is the users themselves who are likely to accidentally delete files or put them in the wrong place! The backup utility is probably the most important one of them all.

- Antivirus software: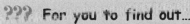

A **virus** is a program that is installed on a computer without your knowledge  or permission with the purpose of doing harm. It includes instructions to replicate automatically on a computer and between computers. Some viruses are just annoying but don't really do any damage but some viruses will delete and/or change system files so work files are corrupted or the computer becomes unusable.

> **??? For you to find out...**
>
> Use the internet to find out about the "I love you" virus, which wreaked havoc in 2000 and inspired a film in 2011.
> How did it infect PCs around the world so quickly?   Who did it affect?

Antivirus software will protect a computer in three ways:

- o   It prevents harmful programs being installed on the computer.

- o   It prevents important files, such as the operating system, being changed or deleted.

- o   If a virus does manage to install itself, the software will detect it when it performs regular scans. Any virus detected will be removed (inoculated!).

New viruses are found regularly so it is important that any antivirus software gets regular updates from the internet.

- Firewall:

If a computer is connected to the internet it is potentially accessible to anyone else on the internet. If a local area network, such as a school network, is connected to the internet then all the file servers, the email server, the web server and all the computers are potentially accessible. Some people hack "just because they can" but often it is for identity theft or just getting your bank account details so they can empty your account. Occasionally people hack with malicious intent but this is less common.

A **firewall** blocks access from the internet onto a PC or network. These work using several factor, for example:

- Where the access is from (the computer's address)
- The type of traffic
- Specific web sites

A firewall doesn't just stop unwanted access from the outside world via the internet; it can also stop computers on a network from accessing specific sites or categories of site on the network. This feature is used to stop staff in companies watching the cricket while they should be working or from using social

networking sites during work hours. In school you'll find that many sites have been blocked. Try going to a games website or getting to Facebook on a school a computer and you will probably get a message saying that the site has been blocked. It is the firewall software that stops this traffic getting out of the local area network and onto the internet.

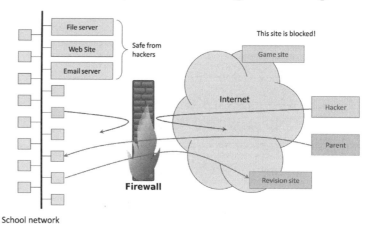

Operating systems like MS Windows have firewall utilities included but you can also buy firewall software separately. Free firewall software can also be downloaded from the internet and many banks provide free firewall software to customers using their internet banking services.

- Spyware protection:

Programs that secretly record what you do on your computer are called **spyware**. The purpose of the software is to capture passwords, bank account details and keywords used in internet shopping and banking. These details can then be used to make purchases on the internet.

A spyware protection utility runs in the background on a PC. It detects spyware programs and prevents them installing. It needs to regularly update itself from the internet so it can detect any new threats.

Some spyware is used for legitimate purposes though. Companies can use spyware to track what is happening on an employee's computer. This is not common and the employee should know it is happening. Parental control software may also use spyware-type programs.

Disk Organisation Utilities

- File transfer & file management:

We take it for granted that we can organise our files into folders and easily move files around within the folder structure. This utility provides a logical view of how the files are organised to make it easier for the user. There are no little yellow folders actually on the disk, just lots of binary!

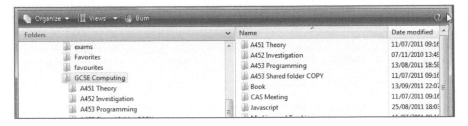

- Disk defragmenter:

The file management utility above makes the secondary storage look like a nicely organised filing cabinet but it doesn't really look like this. Files are stored on the hard disk wherever there is space. If you have a big file it might get split up into sections so it can be stored in the available gaps. This isn't very efficient because the operating system then has to keep track of where all the pieces are. After a while hundreds of files are stored in bits all over the disk. Files have become "fragmented".

The **disk defragmenter** should be run to improve the efficiency of the computer. It moves the separate parts of the files around so they can be stored together. This makes them quicker to access. The defragmenter also groups all the free disk space together so files can be stored in one place. The defragmenter utility optimises disk performance.

Before disk is defragmented, the disk contains lots of files, stored all over the disk:

New file has to be saved in three different parts of the disk. Makes reading the file slower.

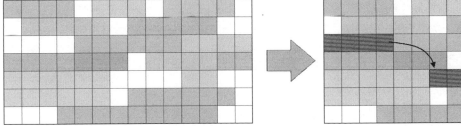

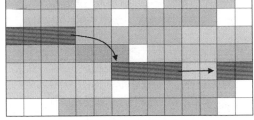

After defragmenting, the disk looks like this:

New file can be saved in one place so speeds up read access.

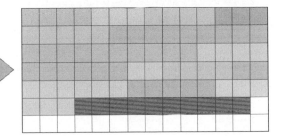

- Formatting:

All storage media (disks, memory sticks etc) need formatting. Mostly we buy portable devices already formatted so you don't have to format a floppy disk or USB memory stick, but hard disks in computers will be formatted by the operating system so they are ready to store files in the way the operating system expects.

Maintenance utilities

- System information and diagnosis:

This is a utility usually provided with the operating system. It gives information about the hardware, statistics about its use and information that will help diagnose any problems with the computer. These are examples of system information and diagnostic screens you might see:

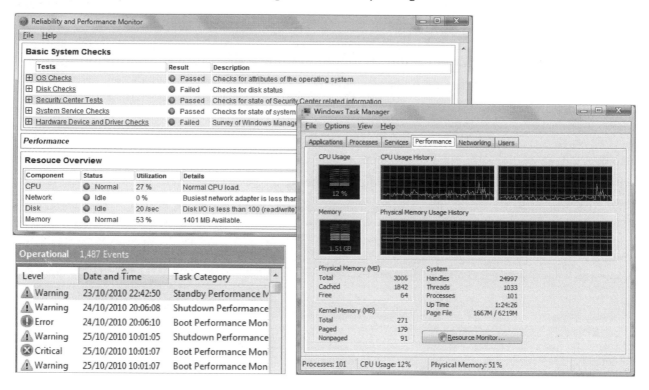

- System cleanup tools:

The system cleanup utility searches for and deletes files that are no longer needed, for example, files that are used to install a software package. Once the package is installed these can be deleted. Also, many temporary files are created when files are moved around on the computer. All temporary files can be deleted to clean-up the disk and improve performance.

Sometimes settings can be wrong or no longer needed. The system cleanup utility will correct errors in settings and delete ones that are no longer needed.

Using the cleanup tools regularly will free up disk space, speed up how quickly the system boots and improve the performance.

- Automatic updating:

The automatic update utility makes sure that any software installed on the computer is up to date. For any software already installed on the computer, the automatic update utility will regularly check on the internet for updates. These will be downloaded and installed if they are newer than the version already on the computer.

For software such as firewalls and antivirus software it is essential that they are updated regularly as new viruses and threats are constantly being devised and discovered.

Application software should also be updated as there will be bug fixes and improvements that become available to people with a license for that package.

Stand-alone utility programs

As well as the utilities we take for granted on our PCs, there are utility programs that can be purchased separately to help manage the computer. The virus protection and firewall software that you use on your computer does not have to be the one provided in the operating system. Many people use a separate package. There are also other utility programs such as compression software or software that converts different types of documents to other formats.

APPLICATION SOFTWARE

The OCR Specification says that you should be able to:

- discuss the relative merits of custom written, off the shelf, open source and proprietary software

This section looks at different ways of sourcing software. We can use software that has already been written for general use but there are different ways of accessing this. Some software is free and some software can be changed to suit our needs but a lot of software is quite expensive and there are restrictions on what we can do with it. If there isn't a package available already we can also get software written specifically for our needs.

Open Source vs Proprietary

Open Source software is governed by the Open Source Initiative that says:

- Software is licensed for use but there is no charge for the **license**. Anyone can use it.
- Open Source software must be distributed with the source code so anyone can modify it.
- Developers can sell the software they have created.
- Any new software created from Open Source software must also be "open". This means that it must be distributed or sold in a form that other people can read and also edit.

NB: This is different from **Freeware** (free software) where it may be free to use but the user does not get access to the source code. Freeware usually has restrictions on its use as well.

Proprietary software is software that is sold as a license to use the software. There will be restrictions on how the software can be used, for example only one concurrent user or up to 50 users on one site (site license). The company or person who wrote the software will hold the copyright. The users will not get access to the source code and will not be allowed to modify the package and sell it to other people. This would break the copyright (Copyright, Designs and Patents Act).

The benefit of using proprietary software is the support available from the company. There will be updates and technical support lines, training courses and a large user base. Open Source software tends to be more organic – it changes over time as developers modify source code and distribute new versions. There isn't a commercial organisation behind the software so there probably won't be a helpline or regular updates, just a community of enthusiastic developers.

Off-the Shelf vs Custom Written Software

 **Off-the-shelf** software is exactly what it sounds like: you can go into a shop and pick it up off the shelf and buy it there and then. Off-the-shelf also applies to applications you buy online as this is essentially the same, without going to the shop. You still get the software within a day or so. This is an application package that someone has written and sold a license to use.

As many people will buy the software you don't have to pay anywhere near the development costs. The company selling the software will make money because so many people buy it. Imagine how many people use Microsoft Word or how many people have bought Norton Antivirus.

> **!!! Interesting fact…**
> In March 2009, statistics were released stating that 15 million people were playing CoD Black Ops!

Commonly used off-the-shelf applications are the everyday packages we use in school, for example, word-processing software, spreadsheets and email.

Advantages of off-the-shelf software:

- You can buy it straight away
- Cheaper than custom written software
- Lots of people use it so there will be plenty of support including help lines, books, user forums, internet sites offering help, training courses
- Regular updates and bug fixes from the company

Disadvantages of off-the-shelf software:

- Made to suit many people so there may be many features that you never use making the software more complicated than it needed to be.

Custom written software is written for a customer to suit their specific requirements. It is not available to the general public. The company developing the software will analyse what the customer needs, design & make the software, and then deliver it. They must charge enough money to cover their development costs and make a profit so the customer will end up paying a lot more for custom software than buying an off-the-shelf package. This whole process takes time. You cannot order the software and expect it to arrive in the next couple of days. Custom software takes months or even years to develop.

Advantages of custom software:

- It does exactly what you want it to do. There might not be an off-the-shelf option for specialist requirements so custom-written software might be the only choice.
- No one else will have the software so it might mean your company can do something others can't or makes you more efficient than your competitors.

Disadvantages of custom software:

- You cannot have it straight away. The software may not be available for months or years.
- It is much more expensive than off-the-shelf software.
- No one else will be using this software so you can't go the local bookshop and buy a "How to…" guide.
- No regular updates and bug fixes to download - the company who wrote the software will charge a lot of money to upgrade the software.

GLOSSARY OF TERMS

Software Categories

Software	Programs that run on the computer.
System software	Programs that are used to run the computer, including the operating system, utilities, library routines and programming language translators.
Application software	Programs that perform a task for a user. This is something that the user would do with or without a computer, it the task that matters not the computer.
Operating system	Systems software that is necessary to run the computer.
Utility programs	System software that provides other useful functions for operating the computer.
Library	Systems software modules that perform frequently required tasks. They can be built into or called from other programs.
Translators	System software that translates high level programming languages into machine code. Includes compilers, interpreters and assemblers.

Operating Systems

Memory management	One of the main functions of the operating system – managing multiple applications using the space in main memory so all programs can be executed efficiently.
Peripheral	A device (hardware) that is connected to the CPU to provide input, output or storage
Peripheral management	One of the main functions of the operating system – managing the input to the CPU and the output from the CPU.
Multi-tasking	One of the main functions of the operating system – managing how several tasks or programs, which are all running at the same time, share the processor.
Security	One of the main functions of the operating system – protecting the computer system from various hazards such as unauthorised users, viruses, hackers and accidental damage.

Operating Systems (continued)

User interface	The method of communication between the computer and its user. Sometimes called HCI (Human-Computer Interface) or MMI (Man-Machine Interface).
HCI	Human-Computer Interface: another term for user interface.
MMI	Man-Machine Interface: another term for user interface.
GUI	Graphical User Interface. A style of user interface, which is based on icons rather than text.
WIMP interface	Stands for: Windows, Icons, Menus & Pointers. It describes a type of user interface where the user selects icons and menu items with a pointer of some kind (with a mouse, stylus or finger).
Command-line interface	A style of user interface that is only text-based. Commands are typed in at a text prompt.
Address	A numerical reference to a location in memory.
Process	A program that is running in main memory.
Single-user	Describes the operating system of a computer where only one person can use the computer at any one time.
Multi-user	Describes the operating system of a computer where more than one person can use the computer at any one time.

Utilities

Virus	A program that is installed on a computer without your knowledge or permission with the purpose of doing harm. It includes instructions to replicate automatically on a computer and between computers.
Antivirus Software	A utility program that prevents harmful programs being installed and important files being changed. If a virus does install itself, the antivirus software detects and removes it.
Firewall	A utility program that prevents unauthorised access to computers or a LAN from the internet and controls what sites computers on the LAN can access.
Spyware	A program that secretly records the user's actions on the computer including passwords and personal details they type when accessing a secure site.

Utilities (continued)

Disk Defragmenter	A utility program that optimises the use of the hard disk space by collecting together the separate parts of each file in one location on the disk as well as grouping together the space so newly saved files do not have to be fragmented (split up).
System Cleanup	A utility program that deletes unnecessary files and settings to optimise the computer's performance.
Automatic Update	A utility program that, for any software already installed on the computer, will regularly check on the internet for newer versions and updates, download and install them.
System Information and Diagnosis	A utility program that presents information about the computer hardware and usage as well as information to help diagnose problems.
Formatting	A utility program that formats secondary storage devices such as hard disks.
File transfer & file management	A utility program that allows the user to create a logical view of how their files are organised using folders. Allows the user to move files within folders, copy, paste, name and delete files.

Applications

Open Source	Software that is provided under license but free of charge to anyone. The source code is made available and can be modified.
License	An agreement that defines the conditions for using the software.
Freeware	Software that is provided free of charge under license but without the source code. It is copyrighted and cannot be modified.
Proprietary software	Software that is copyrighted and the license is sold under a patented or trademarked name.
Off-the-shelf software	Software that can be purchased from a high street or online store as it is. Not custom-written.
Custom written software	Software that is written for a customer's specific requirements, just for that customer.

PAST EXAM QUESTIONS & EXAMPLE ANSWERS

From the specimen paper

5   Ali's new computer uses a single-user, multi-tasking operating system.

(a)   What is a **single-user** operating system?

Only one person can use the computer at any one time   [2]

(b)   What is a **multi-tasking** operating system?

The computer can appear to run several programs at the same time.

For example, using the word processor while downloading a podcast and playing

a music file.   [2]

(c)   Ali wants to know which utility programs he will need to keep his computer secure and running smoothly.

Discuss the utility programs Ali will need, justifying why he needs them.

The quality of written communication will be assessed in your answer to this question.

To keep his computer secure, Ali should use the following utilities:

*   *Antivirus software: If his computer is connected to the internet he may be vulnerable to viruses from web pages or emails. The antivirus software will regularly check his files, detect any viruses and delete them.*

*   *Firewall: This will stop unauthorised access to his computer from the internet so hackers won't be able to look at his personal files.*

*   *Automatic update: to keep his virus and firewall software current his computer would need to be downloading the updates and new virus definitions regularly.*

To keep his computer running smoothly Ali should use:

*   *Disk defragmenter: This will keep all the files together and free up larger blocks of space for new files. This will improve the computer's performance because files can be accessed quicker.*

*   *Disk cleanup: This will delete files and settings his computer no longer needs so free up more space.*   [6]

From Jan 2011 Paper

5 Karen wants to use handheld computers to take customers' orders in her restaurant. She is thinking of using custom written, open source software.

(a) State what is meant by custom written software.

Software that is written for the customer's (Karen's) specific requirements.

(b) State two reasons why Karen may decide to use custom written software.

1. *There is no off-the-shelf software package to do what Karen wants*

2. *The off-the-shelf packages available do not do exactly what Karen wants*   [2]

(c) Discuss the implications of creating open source software for the restaurant.

The quality of written communication will be assessed in your answer to this question.

If Karen gets someone to create custom software for her using a similar Open Source program it will make the custom development cheaper and quicker. Her developer will be able to modify similar source code, which is free, to create a custom solution for Karen's restaurant. However, she will then have to make her source code available to others as Open Source is about collaboration and sharing. Karen may object to sharing her code with others but in this case it is unlikely; she is only using the software to take orders so she is unlikely to be getting any serious competitive advantage from it.

Open source software is free so Karen will only have to pay for the customisation. Overall the cost will be less than starting the program from scratch. She could even sell the product to other restaurants, which may have a similar need to get some money back.

With a large number of Open Source developers around Karen may find it easy to get changes made later but she has no guarantees of the quality of the product she is buying.   [6]

CHAPTER 5:   DATABASES

This topic looks at the basic concept of a database, the key features and benefits of a Database Management System (DBMS) and the basic theory behind relational databases such as Microsoft Access. Using Microsoft Access is a good way to get practical experience of relational database concepts and the features of a DBMS. This chapter does not provide instruction on how to use any one DBMS package but provides an overview of the theory required for the GCSE exam.

THE DATABASE CONCEPT

The OCR Specification says that you should be able to:

- describe a database as a persistent organised store of data
- explain the use of data handling software to create, maintain and interrogate a database

Many organisations keep large amounts of data. A company will store data about its customers and staff, schools store data about the students, supermarkets store data about stock levels and customer buying patterns. This data could be stored in books, card files or spreadsheets, depending on the volume and type of data. When there are large quantities of data an organisation is most likely to use a database.

A **database** is described as "**a persistent organised store of data**". Let's look at each part of that definition:

- **"Store of data"** :
  Clearly lots of data are being stored in a database.

- **"Organised"** :
  A database is more than just a store of data.
  A graphics file or collection of post-it notes on a wall is a "collection of data". A database has the data organised into **records**. A school database will have a record per student for example.

- **"Persistent"** :
  This means that a database is a non-volatile store of data on a secondary storage medium such as a hard disk. This is in comparison to an array, which could also be described as an organised store of data but an array only exists in memory while a program is running. A database exists on a disk and can be accessed by a program but the database itself is in persistent storage.

> **!!! NB...**
> Data is a plural term so "...data are..." is not a grammar mistake!
> The singular is "datum".

Data Handling Software

Data handling software can be created using an off-the-shelf product such as Microsoft Access or MySQL. Alternatively you can create the database itself in one of these products and program a forms-based front-end application in a high level programming language such as Delphi or Visual Basic.

A database must first be created. The data must be gathered and organised in some way. Consider a company that wants a database for all its products. They will need a **record** for each product that stores all the relevant details about that product. The specific details will be stored as **fields**. Fields for a product database might include ProductID, Description, Supplier, Price, NumberInStock etc Please notice the lack of spaces in these field names – just like in programming, it is considered good practice to use Pascal Case to name fields (see p111, Chapter 7, "Programming").

A spreadsheet table is a basic database and could look like this:

	A	B	C	D	E
1	ProductID	Description	Supplier	Price	NumberInStock
2	0123	Humbugs, 250g bag	Smiths & Sons	£1.45	200
3	0263	Toffee, small slab	Old Fashioned Toffee	£1.75	34
4	0462	Lemon Sherbets, 500g bag	Smiths & Sons	£2.50	128
5	1234	Lemon Sherbets, 250g bag	Smiths & Sons	£1.75	134

This database contains the basic information that the company needs about product pricing and stock levels. The applications that use this data will **interrogate** the database. Interrogate means to ask questions about the data or to **query** it. For example, how many products have a stock level below 50 and need reordering? Or, how much does a bag of humbugs cost?

The quality of the information you get from a database application is only as good as the data you put in: GIGO is an acronym for Garbage In, Garbage Out! A database must be **maintained**. This means that when the data changes in the real world, the database must be updated to make sure the data stored is correct and up-to-date.

A database can be considered in terms of its life history and the operations that can be performed on it:

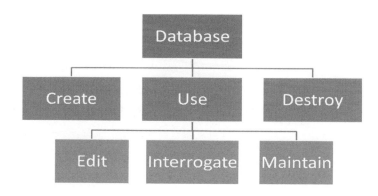

THE DBMS

The OCR Specification says that you should be able to:

- describe how a DBMS allows the separation of data from applications and why this is desirable
- describe the principal features of a DBMS and how they can be used to create customised data handling applications

The traditional approach to storing data in a company was for everyone to store their own data in their own files.

A company might have a Sales department dealing with customers, an Accounts department that dealt with the same customers when they bought things and a Training department that trained the same customers on the products they'd just bought. Traditionally all of these departments would have kept their own data files, rather than sharing one file of data.

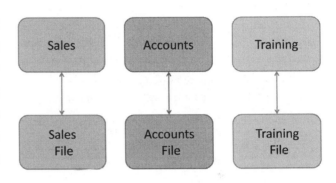

The problem with this approach is that there are three copies of the same customer details. When a customer moves house he phones the sales person and assumes that the rest of company now has his new address. In practice, the Sales department had the up-to-date details but the rest of company didn't. This is called "data inconsistency" and is the main problem with duplicating data in more than one place. This is easily solved by everyone sharing one database instead of using their own files.

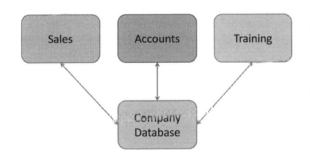

In computer systems we always try to avoid duplicating data in more than one place. So remember:

Data duplication leads to data inconsistency

The problem with this approach was that each department wanted to do different things with the data. They all had their own departmental applications. Sharing the data meant that it was now consistent but introduced security issues and issues with the applications being closely linked to the data. If the Sales department changed something in the database then it affected the programs that other departments were using. The applications were too closely tied to the database. There needed to be some separation between the programs and the data they were using.

The separation of the programs from the data is achieved using a **database management system** (**DBMS**). This is a software system that provides controlled access to the database. This separation is sometimes called **program-data independence**.

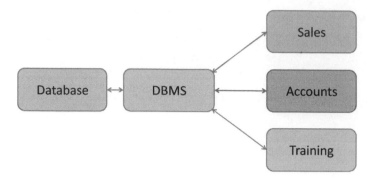

Some key features of a database management system are:

- Provide separation between the applications and the database

- Allow multiple applications to use a single database

- Manage multiple applications trying to edit the same record at the same time (usually makes it read-only for second application)

- Provides appropriate **views** of the database to different users

- Provides security in terms of views and access rights

- Enables the creation of the relational database structure

- Allows applications to query/interrogate the database

- Enables the creation of reports based on queries

- Allows the applications to edit and maintain the database (with appropriate access rights)

- Can provide automatic backups if required

The DBMS that you are most likely to use is Microsoft Access. It provides all of the features above to create a customised data handling application.

The next section of this chapter discusses the components of a relational database structure and the DBMS components used to create the application that uses it.

??? For you to find out...

Microsoft Access is very popular in schools and small businesses but what other Database Management Systems are there?

Find another three examples of DBMS.

RELATIONAL DATABASES

The OCR Specification says that you should be able to:

- understand the relationship between entities and tables
- understand the components of a relational database, such as tables, forms, queries, reports and modules
- understand the use of logical operators in framing database queries
- explain the use of key fields to connect tables and avoid data redundancy
- describe methods of validating data as it is input

As we saw earlier in the chapter a database is a persistent organised store of data. The example of product details in a spreadsheet is a type of database. If you store all your data in a single file or worksheet it is called a **flat file**. This might be fine for simple data storage but as companies need to store more and more data problems start to occur.

The spreadsheet (flat file) below stores student details. Every student belongs to a tutor group that is either a "6th form" tutor group or a "block" tutor group (year 9 to 11). Notice that all of the details about Susan Robson's tutor group are repeated for every student in her tutor group. This is duplicated data and, as we said earlier, this can lead to data inconsistency later. If Susan's tutor group moves rooms then several students' records would need to be updated. It is too easy to miss one and end up with inconsistent data.

	A	B	C	D	E	F	G	H	I	J	K	L
1	Candidate number	First Name	Surname	Address 1	Address 2	Town	County	Postcode	Tutor Group	Tutor name	Type	Room
2	0001	Fred	Smith	23 The Road		Basingstoke	Hampshire	RG22 3FG	SJR	Susan Robson	6th Form	IT1
3	0002	Sally	Jones	32 Pleasant Street		Basingstoke	Hampshire	RG23 4SD	RLH	Jane Hobson	6th Form	120
4	0003	George	Dotts	345 Boundary Lane		Reading	Berkshire	RG1 4CV	RLH	Jane Hobson	6th Form	120
5	0004	Joyce	Handel	2 Pickle Avenue		Reading	Berkshire	RG2 8NM	SJR	Susan Robson	6th Form	IT1
6	0005	Mabel	Pickles	The Old Post Office	Church Lane	Guildford	Surrey	GU8 5GT	SJR	Susan Robson	6th Form	IT1
7	0006	Harry	Simpson	45 Foundary Road		Basingstoke	Hampshire	RG24 6YU	PLT	Paula Harris	Block	123
8	0007	Xander	Erikson	Flat 3	Box Row	Reading	Berkshire	RG3 2SD	RLH	Jane Hobson	6th Form	120
9	0008	Arnold	Holland	45 Reading Road		Guildford	Surrey	GU1 5TY	PLT	Paula Harris	Block	123
10	0009	Lester	Jakes	567 Tower Street		Basingstoke	Hampshire	RG23 4WQ	JKS	Jonathan Simpkins	Block	011
11	0010	Jasmin	Flood	3a The Cottages	Dover Street	Basingstoke	Hampshire	RG24 7BN	JKS	Jonathan Simpkins	Block	011

In computing we aim to store each piece of data just once. Ideally we should separate the data stored about tutor groups and the data stored about students. We only need to know which tutor group each student is in. We can refer to the other table to find out more details of that tutor group.

	A	B	C	D	E	F	G	H	I	J	K	L	M	N
1	Candidate number	First Name	Surname	Address 1	Address 2	Town	County	Postcode	Tutor Group		Tutor Group	Tutor name	Type	Room
2	0001	Fred	Smith	23 The Road		Basingstoke	Hampshire	RG22 3FG	SJR		SJR	Susan Robson	6th Form	IT1
3	0002	Sally	Jones	32 Pleasant Street		Basingstoke	Hampshire	RG23 4SD	RLH		RLH	Jane Hobson	6th Form	120
4	0003	George	Dotts	345 Boundary Lane		Reading	Berkshire	RG1 4CV	RLH		PLT	Paula Harris	Block	123
5	0004	Joyce	Handel	2 Pickle Avenue		Reading	Berkshire	RG2 8NM	SJR		JKS	Jonathan Simpkins	Block	011
6	0005	Mabel	Pickles	The Old Post Office	Church Lane	Guildford	Surrey	GU8 5GT	SJR					
7	0006	Harry	Simpson	45 Foundary Road		Basingstoke	Hampshire	RG24 6YU	PLT					
8	0007	Xander	Erikson	Flat 3	Box Row	Reading	Berkshire	RG3 2SD	RLH					
9	0008	Arnold	Holland	45 Reading Road		Guildford	Surrey	GU1 5TY	PLT					

Reducing data duplication (data redundancy) has several benefits:

- reduces the risk of data inconsistency
- makes maintaining the database much easier
- reduces the size of the database

To understand relational databases there is no substitute for making one yourself. Use Microsoft Access to create your own relational database and application (forms, queries and reports). The following sections look at the basic theory.

Creating a Relational Database

A relational database is a collection of data stored in related tables. In the real-world there are objects and people that we store data about. These are called **entities**. In the spreadsheet example on the previous page we modelled two entities, "student" and "tutor group".

In a relational database we create a table for each entity so a table is a collection of data about a specific entity. We use a database management system such as Microsoft Access to create these tables and to create logical links between them, **relationships**.

Here is the spreadsheet example from earlier in the chapter, recreated as tables in Access. There are two entities, student and tutor group so we create a table for each. This avoids storing the same data twice (avoids redundancy). Notice that the tutor group initials appear against each student so we know which tutor group they are in. This same field also appears in the TutorGroup table so we can then reference the tutor group details. These fields have a special function in the database; they are used to create a **relationship** between the two tables.

Both Sally and George are in tutor group "JLH". This field connects the Student table to the TutorGroup table so the tutor group details can be accessed. From the two related tables we can see that Sally and George both go to classroom 120 for tutor time.

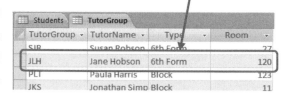

Each table contains records for each student or each tutor group. The records are made up of fields, individual data items such as "surname" or "town". With potentially hundreds or thousands of records it is critical that the computer can tell which one is which so every record must have a unique identifier. The field that uniquely identifies each record in a table is called the **primary key**.

The primary key can be a number or text but every record must have a different value for this field. In the example above the primary key for the student table is "CandidateNumber". The primary key for the TutorGroup table is "TutorGroup" (the tutor's initials in this case).

In Access, the relationship between the two tables appears like this:

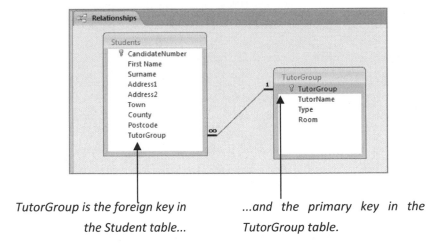

TutorGroup is the foreign key in   ...and the primary key in the
the Student table...   TutorGroup table.

It shows the two tables and the fields they contain. It shows the primary key fields in each table with the key symbol. It also shows the relationship created between the two tables. Be aware that you can only create a relationship from one table to the primary key field of another. The field used is called the **foreign key**.

Using Forms to Add/Edit Data

Having created the database itself (the collection of related tables) the data must be entered. This can be imported from another file such as a spreadsheet or typed into the table, one record at a time. Once the database is in use the user will need to be able to add new records, delete records and edit existing records.

In Microsoft Access the user can be given direct access to the tables but normally they would have a forms-based application interface to protect the database from user errors.

Forms can easily be created with a DBMS to allow controlled access to the underlying database. Remember that there may be several different applications using the same data and that each type of user will need different types of access. Some people will be allowed to see and edit all of the data but others may only be able to view it or access reports based on it. One of the strengths of a DBMS is that it can offer different types of user different views.

The form to the right is a typical form made in Microsoft Access to add new Tutor Groups to the database.

Having created a form that allows users to easily input data we can also add **validation** to check that the data being entered is reasonable. In this case we know that the school numbers its rooms with 3 digits so we can check that the room number is between 1 and 999 (a range check). If the user enters something else then they get an error message. This protects the integrity of the data.

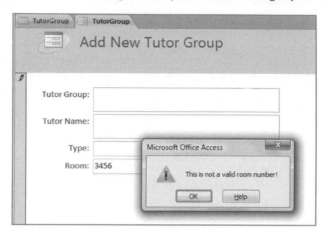

The screen shot below shows another type of validation where the user is forced to pick options from a list (combo-box) so that they cannot enter any other variations by mistake:

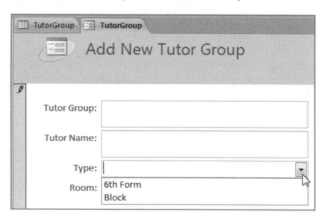

Validation is when the computer software checks that the data entered is reasonable or sensible and conforms to rules about the type of data allowed. There are several types of validation that are used when creating an application:

- **Range check**: a number or date is within a sensible/allowed range
- **Type check**: data is the right type such as an integer or a letter or text
- **Length check**: text entered is not too long or too short, for example: a password is greater than 8 characters, a product description is no longer than 25 characters
- **Existence check**: checks that a product or customer exists in the database, for example: if an order is being entered in a system it checks if that product actually exists in the database
- **Presence check**: checks that some data has been entered, that is has not been left blank
- **Format check**: checks that the format is appropriate such as a postcode or email address

Validation can only check if data is reasonable. It cannot tell if it is correct. This is an important differentiation. If the "Student's Details" form prompts for Date of Birth the application can check that the data entered would be appropriate for that age group, it cannot tell if you enter November instead of December by mistake.

Whilst validation ensures that the data entered are sensible, **verification** double checks that it has been typed in correctly. This is where data is entered twice and the two versions are compared. If they are different the user can be prompted to try again. This is commonly used where email addresses and passwords are entered on forms.

Using Queries to Interrogate the Database

Stored data is only as useful as what you do with it. Once data has been stored in a database the users need to be able to find out things about it and generate reports.

Queries are used to interrogate the database. With a student database you may need to find a specific student's contact details or get a list of all the students in a particular class, for example. A DBMS will allow you to construct queries that find data matching specified criteria. In Microsoft Access the Query By Example (QBE) grid makes it easy to find records that match criteria. Here is an example:

Query to find all students that live in Hampshire:

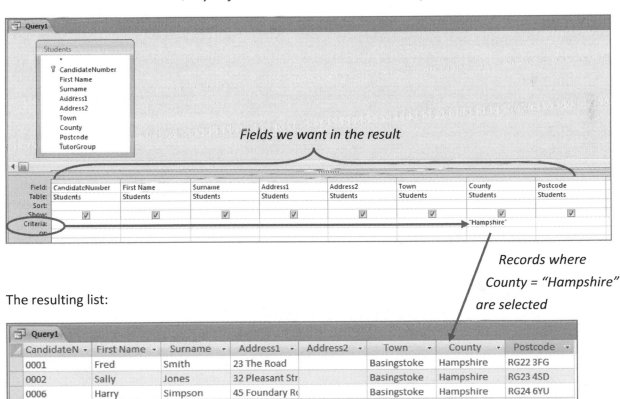

The resulting list:

In an exam you will need to be able to write criteria to select specific records. Some of these will include more than one part and some logical operators (NOT, AND, OR). Here are some examples:

`CandidateNumber="0010"`   selects the details for that specific candidate

`(County="Hampshire") AND (TutorGroup="SJR")`   selects students in tutor group SJR who live in Hamsphire

Notice that each part of the criteria is in brackets where there is more than one part. Just like BIDMAS in mathematical calculations, there is also an order of precedence for logical operators. AND takes precedence over OR so you may need extra brackets if the OR parts need resolving first:

`(County="Hampshire") AND (TutorGroup="SJR")OR (TutorGroup="JLH")`

The criteria above will return students from tutor group SJR who also live in Hampshire and all the students in tutor group JLH.

`(County="Hampshire") AND ((TutorGroup="SJR") OR (TutorGroup="JLH"))`

This version, with the OR parts bracketed, will return students who are in either of these tutor groups who also live in Hampshire!

Using Reports to Present Information

Data are just facts and figures with no context. They can be processed into reports to convey information. Information is processed data that has context and meaning. A DBMS can take data from tables or the results of queries and present them in reports. Here is an example of a report produced in Access:

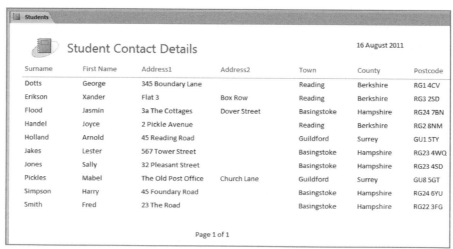

A good report should always be dated, have a clear title, be laid out clearly and have page numbers. In some cases you would expect the information to be sorted into a particular order. Lists of people tend be sorted alphabetically by surname, a price list would be sorted by product ID number. Sometimes data is grouped within a report and there may be subtotals and totals of numerical amounts. Company reports will generally be done in a "house-style" and include the company logo.

Customising Your Application Using Code

However good the features of a DBMS are, there is always something else you want to tailor. Most database management systems provide a programming interface so you can write code. The code is stored in **modules**.

Here is an example of a validation routine written in Visual Basic for Applications (VBA), the programming language within Microsoft Access. It checks that email addresses have an @ symbol and a dot in them:

```
Private Sub txtEmailAddress_Exit(Cancel As Integer)
  Dim AtPosn As Integer
  Dim DotPosn As Integer

  If Len(txtEmailAddress.Text) < 5 Then
    MsgBox "Email address is too short!"
  Else
    AtPosn = InStr(txtEmailAddress.Text, "@")
    If AtPosn < 2 Then
      MsgBox "Invalid email address, need characters before @"
    Else
      DotPosn = InStr(AtPosn, txtEmailAddress.Text, ".")
      If DotPosn = 0 Then
        MsgBox "Invalid email address, need at least 1 dot after @"
      End If
    End If
  End If
End Sub
```

This code tailors the form to validate the email address and generate error messages as follows:

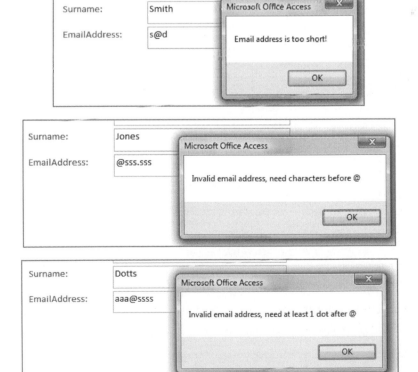

GLOSSARY OF TERMS

Database Concepts

Database	A persistent organised store of data.
Persistent Storage	Non-volatile storage on a secondary storage medium such as a hard disk.
Data Duplication / Data Redundancy	Where the same data is stored more than once, unnecessarily.
Data Inconsistency	Where different versions of data become different because duplicate versions have been stored and updated differently.
Program-Data Independence	Where the applications that use a shared database are separated from the actual data by a database management system. Changes can be made to one application without it affecting another.
DBMS	Stands for Database Management System, the system that separates the applications from the data and provides features that allow database systems to be created, interrogated and maintained.
Views	A feature of a DBMS that provides each application or user with specific access rights and views of the database.

Relational Databases

Flat File Database	A persistent organised store of data where data is stored in a single file organised into fields and records.
Relational Database	A persistent organised store of data where data is stored as a collection of related tables to minimise data redundancy.
Entity	A real world object, about which data is stored in a database, corresponds to a table in the relational database.
Table	A collection of data organised into records and fields within a relational database. A table represents a real-world entity.

Relational Databases (continued)

Record	Data stored about one instance of an entity ie: one particular person or object.
Field	One specific data item being stored such as surname or shoe size.
Primary Key	A field in a table that uniquely identifies a record.
Foreign Key	A field in one table that is the primary key in another table and is used to create a relationship between those two tables.
Relationship	The logical connection created between two tables using a primary and foreign key pair.
Form	An interactive window used for data entry. Usually includes validation routines.
Validation	When the computer software checks that data entered is sensible.
Verification	Where data is entered twice and checked that each version is the same, to avoid data being entered with typing mistakes.
Queries	A feature of a DBMS that allows the database to be interrogated. It selects records from the database based on specified criteria.
Logical Operator	NOT, AND, OR. Used in complex criteria in queries.
Reports	Data from a database that has been processed and presented on a page in a way that makes it information. Designed for hardcopy.
Modules	Sections of code within a DBMS that allow the user interface to be tailored.

PAST EXAM QUESTIONS & EXAMPLE ANSWERS

From the specimen paper

11   A dentist uses a database to store the details of patients and their appointments.

   (a)   A database management system (DBMS) is used which includes forms, queries and reports.

   Tick one box in each row to show whether each of the following statements best describes a form, a query or a report.

	Form	Query	Report
This can be used to print out all the appointments that the dentist has booked.			✓
This can be used to enter a patient's details when the patient registers with the dentist.	✓		
This can be used to find out all the appointments that a certain patient has made.		✓	

[3]

   (b)   When a patient makes an appointment, the start time of the appointment needs to be validated.

   State two validation checks which can be carried out on the start time of the appointment.

   Check 1   *Format check: the time is in the required format such as hh:mm*

   Check 2   *Range check: the hours part of the time is in the range 0 - 24, the minutes part is in*
   the range 0 – 59   [2]

   (c)   Explain why the patient and the appointment data should be stored as separate entities.

   A patient's details should only be stored once to avoid data redundancy.

   A patient can have several appointments in the appointment table...
   ... linked to the patient details by the PatientID field.

   When an appointment is made the patient's details do not need to be typed in again, just the
   PatientID.   [3]

From Jan 2011 Paper

7   A teacher uses a database to store the marks of pupils from all year 9 classes.

   (a)   PUPIL and CLASS are two entities used in this database.

         Explain the term entity.

         An entity is a real world object about which data is stored in a database.

         Entities become tables in the database.

                                                                              [2]

   (b)   The data for the first four pupils in the PUPIL table is shown below.

PupilNumber	Surname	FirstName	ClassCode
A01	Adams	Michelle	9DK
A02	Ali	Mohammed	9BH
A03	Ali	Shirelle	9DK
A04	Azor	Michelle	9FT

   (i)   State the primary key for the PUPIL table and explain your answer.

         Primary Key   *PupilNumber*   [1]

         Explanation

         The PupilNumber field uniquely identifies each pupil record in the table.

         Pupils may have the same name but they cannot have the same pupil number.   [2]

   (ii)   The database also contains a CLASS table. The primary key for the CLASS table is ClassCode.

          Explain why ClassCode has also been included in the PUPIL table.

          ClassCode is the field that is being used to link a pupil to a class.

          ClassCode is the foreign key in the Pupil table.

          The class details can be accessed by following the link to the Class table   [3]

CHAPTER 6:   NETWORKS

This topic looks at the basics of local and wide area networks. It looks at the internet as an example of a wide area network and some of the technologies associated with networks.

LOCAL AREA NETWORKS (LAN)

A **Local Area Network** (LAN) is defined as a collection of computers and peripheral devices (such as printers) connected together within a single site. Notice that it is within a single <u>site</u> and not a single building. At school you probably have many different buildings within a campus. The school's LAN will connect computers together in all these buildings.

> The OCR Specification says that you should be able to:
>
> • explain the advantages of networking stand-alone computers into a local area network

Consider how you work on a single laptop or PC at home that is not connected to a network. Compare this to how you work on computers at school, which are all on a LAN. A network in a large office building will provide all the same features that you have at school.

Benefits of Networking Computers

The benefits of networking the computers fall into these categories:

- Sharing resources:
    - Sharing folders and files so you can access files anywhere on the network from any computer and different people can access these files as needed.
    - Sharing peripheral devices such as printers and scanners
    - Sharing an internet connection

- Communication:
    - Using email to communicate with colleagues
    - Using messaging systems to chat while you are working on other things
    - Transferring files between computers

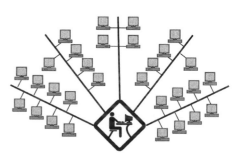

- Centralised management:
    - User profiles and security can all be managed centrally
    - Software can be distributed across the network rather than having to install it on each individual computer
    - Users can use any PC on the network but still see their own files

Network Topologies

Computers can be connected together in different layouts, or topologies. There are three basic topologies that are used but these may be combined in a large network.

- **Bus Network:**

Computers are connected to a single backbone cable. The computers all share this cable to transmit

to each other but only one computer can transmit at any one time. This is fine most of the time if the network is not too busy but if there is a lot of traffic then transmissions interfere with each other and computers have to retransmit.

Advantages:	Disadvantages:
1. Easy and inexpensive to install – less cabling than in a star network	1. If the main cable fails then the whole network goes down
2. Easy to add new computers	2. Cable failures are hard to isolate because it affects all of the computers attached
	3. Performance slows down as the amount of traffic increases

- **Ring Network:**

Computers are connected to adjacent computers in a ring. Computers take it in turns to transmit, controlled by passing a token around the ring. Computers can only transmit when they have the token.
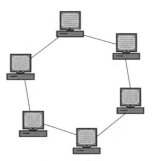

Advantages:	Disadvantages:
1. Not dependent on a central computer like the star network	1. A single node or link failure and the network is disrupted
2. Token passing protocol is simple and therefore reliable	
3. Consistent performance even when there is a lot of traffic	

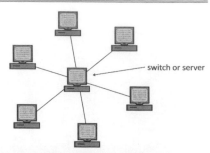

- **Star Network**:

    All of the computers have their own cable that connects them to a central computer. The central computer controls the network. This is usually a server, where shared resources are stored.

Advantages:	Disadvantages:
1. If one cable fails only one station is affected rather than the whole network	1. Can be costly to install because there is a lot of cabling
2. Consistent performance even when the network is heavily used	2. Dependence on a central computer, if it fails then the whole network goes down
3. Easy to add new computers	
4. More secure – messages from a computer go directly to the centre	

Connecting Computers to the LAN

Each computer must have a network card so it can be connected to the LAN. The correct term for the network card is **Network Interface Card** (NIC). The right type must be fitted for the kind of network connection required, either by a cable or wirelessly to the network.

In most classrooms or offices, computers tend be star wired to a hub or switch, which is either in the room or nearby. The room layout may look like a bus network because the cables all go around the edge of the room but in actual fact, each computer has its own wire running through the ducting to the central device.

Smaller star or bus networks in rooms/offices will then be connected to a backbone that could also be a star or a bus topology. In a modern network there will be a mixture of topologies.

The central devices in a small star network may be a server. In an office or classroom on a bigger LAN, the central device in a star will be a switch.

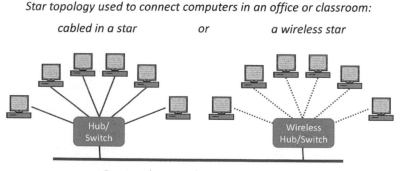

Star topology used to connect computers in an office or classroom:

cabled in a star   or   a wireless star

Bus topology used to connect routers

Peer-to-Peer or Client-Server

In your school you will be able to use your files on computers in different buildings. This is because they are not stored on the computer that you are using but are on a file **server** somewhere else in school. The file server is a specialised computer with a different role to the normal PC. There will also be an email server and a web server on the network.

Client Server Configuration

• *Client computers communicate via central server*
• *Files and email stored centrally*
• *Network managed centrally*

In a large network it is common to have shared files and resources on centralised servers. The computers that you use around school are referred to as **clients**.

The advantage of a client-server network is that management is centralised and clients are not dependent on other clients, just the server.

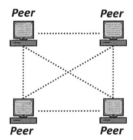

Peer-to-Peer Configuration

• *Peer computers communicate directly with each other*
• *Files stored in individual computers but shared with others*

In smaller offices this is not practical. If you run a small company with a handful of computers it is not cost-effective to have a specialised server or someone to run the network. In a small office the computers will simply be cabled together. Each computer is configured so it will share specified files and folders with other peer computers on the LAN. PCs on the LAN can only access files on another computer if access rights have been granted. This is called a peer-to-peer network because all of the computers have equal status and the same role in the network.

NB: The dotted lines in these diagrams show how the devices communicate with each other, not physical connectivity.

Peer-to-Peer	Client-Server
All computers have equal status	Specialised roles: computers tend to be a client or a server.
Easy to set up and maintain	Needs a network manager to run the network
No centralised management	Centralised security and management
Backup each computer separately	Backup done from central server
No dependency on a server	Dependent on central server

WIDE AREA NETWORKS (WAN)

The OCR Specification says that you should be able to:

- describe the differences between a local area network and a wide area network such as the internet

We said in the last section that a LAN was a collection of computers connected together within a single site. A Wide Area Network, or WAN, is a collection of computers and networks over a geographically remote area.

The term "geographically remote" is a confusing one. It does mean that networks have to be miles apart, although they may be. Geographical remoteness is more about what separates sites than the distance involved. However, the internet is a WAN and this is worldwide. At your school there will be a LAN that connects computers in various buildings. Your campus may be quite large but it is still a LAN. If you have a split campus with a public highway or some other buildings in between the two campuses, then these will need to be connected by a WAN.

WANs use hired infrastructure to connect the LANs together; the school or business cannot install its own cables between the two sites. A business with offices in London, Leeds, Bristol and York will lease connections from a network service provider to connect the four office LANs together.

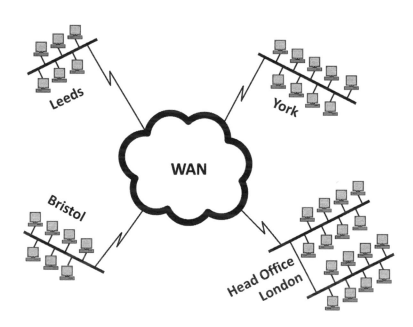

HOW DEVICES COMMUNICATE ON A NETWORK

> The OCR Specification says that you should be able to:
>
> - explain the terms IP addressing, MAC addressing, packet and protocols

Consider how you communicate as a human being. *Buna ziua, ce mai faci azi?* Sorry, don't you speak Romanian?! When we go aboard we find it hard to communicate because we do not understand the language. Even if you can speak French you probably struggle in France because they talk too fast for us to understand. Computer communication has similar problems. Computers need to be speaking the same language and at the same speed in order to communicate.

If one computer transmits a stream of binary to another computer, the receiving end needs to know what the rules are. This is called a **protocol**. A protocol is the set of rules that define how devices communicate. A protocol will cover:

- how the communication will start, getting the attention of the other computer ("Oi, you!")
- the transmission speed
- the significance of the bits being transmitted (like the language)
- how the bits will be delivered (one at a time or in groups of 8 for example)
- error checking procedures being used (this involves some extra bits, like punctuation!).

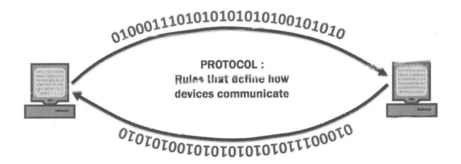

Internet Protocol (IP)

One protocol that you may have heard of is IP. This is the protocol used on the internet. All computers and servers connected to the internet, as well as the routers that make up the internet, communicate using IP.

Internet Protocol will be discussed in more detail in the following section about the internet.

MAC Addresses

If devices are going to communicate they must have a unique reference number. This is called an address. It is the same principal as addressing a letter; you need to put a unique address on the front so the postman knows where to deliver it. Within a LAN each device must have a Network Interface Card (NIC) to connect it to the network. This card will have a **MAC address**. The MAC address is hard-coded into the NIC when it is manufactured, it cannot be configured in software. Every networked device will have a MAC address. It is a 48-bit address that is written as twelve hex digits to make it easier for humans to work with. For example:

```
In hex:     00-09-7C-F1-F7-85

In binary: 000000000000100101111100111100011111011110000101
```

The MAC address is used to transmit between devices within a LAN.

Packets

When two devices want to communicate across a LAN one device will send a **message** to the other. This message is broken into smaller chunks called **packets**. These packets are broadcast onto the LAN with the MAC address of the destination device. The destination device will see all of the traffic on the LAN but will only pick up the packets with its own MAC address on them. It's a bit like getting your luggage back after a flight - you watch all the bags go around on the conveyer belt but you only pick up the one with your name on the label.

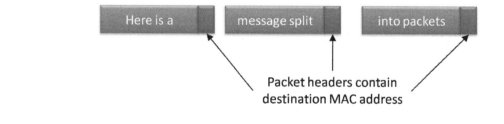

Packet headers contain
destination MAC address

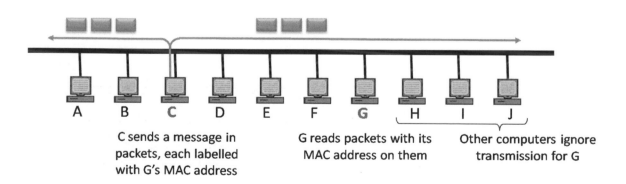

| C sends a message in packets, each labelled with G's MAC address | G reads packets with its MAC address on them | Other computers ignore transmission for G |

THE INTERNET

The OCR Specification says that you should be able to:

- describe the nature of the internet as a worldwide collection of computer networks
- explain the need for IP addressing of resources on the internet and how this can be facilitated by the role of DNS servers

The internet is a wide area network. It is a worldwide collection of computers and networks that uses Internet Protocol (IP) to communicate. It isn't owned or managed by any one group of people and anyone can access it.

The network itself is made up of network devices called **routers**. These are much bigger, higher performance routers than the ones at school or at home. They form the backbone of the network. IP is the protocol used between these routers.

Internet Protocol (IP)

Each device on the internet must have a unique IP address so they can communicate over the wide area. This is in addition to the hardware MAC address, which is only used to address devices inside a LAN. The IP address is made up of four numbers separated by three dots, for example: 193.127.30.23

The four numbers each represent a byte so each one can only be a number between 0 and 255. The computers will be sending binary, not decimal integers, but we write the addresses as four separate numbers because it is easier for a people to deal with. (The dots are not transmitted; they are just separators to make it easier for us to read.)

$$11000001 \quad 01111111 \quad 00011110 \quad 00010111$$

$$193. \qquad 127. \qquad 30. \qquad 23$$

Some IP addresses have special significance and are not used for devices. For example, 0.0.0.0 and 255.255.255.255 are never used to address a device.

Accessing Websites on the Internet

Websites are stored on web servers connected to the internet. The site will have an IP address so people can access the pages using their browser software. However, when

you want to access a site you don't type the IP address, you type in a **domain name** such as www.bbc.co.uk. This is because humans are quite bad at remembering numbers and typing them in correctly so the domain name is a text reference to a site that can be translated into the numerical IP address.

When you type the domain name, "www.microsoft.com" into the browser the web page request is sent to a **Domain Name System (DNS) server** in the internet. The DNS server has a database of domain names and IP addresses so it can translate the domain name into an IP address.

There are a large number of DNS servers in the internet and these communicate with each other so the DNS servers regularly update each other. If your local DNS server does not have the domain name listed, the page request can be forwarded to another DNS server.

The advantages of using DNS servers to translate domain names into IP addresses are:

- Humans do not have to remember or type in numerical addresses
- If the IP addresses change at some point the DNS servers can update their databases, the users can continue using the same domain names.
- Many distributed DNS servers means everyone has access to all addresses from their local DNS server.

In most browsers you can also type the IP address of a site into the address bar to get to a site. We don't tend to do this but it shows that essentially the domain name and IP address both address the same place. This IP address gets you to the Microsoft home page:

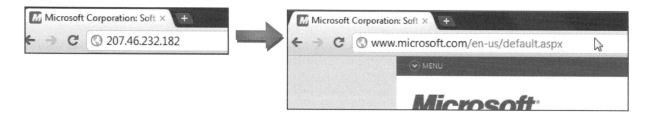

You may also have noticed that your browser adds "http://" in front of the domain name you typed.

This is another example of a protocol. **HTTP** stands for **Hyper Text Transfer Protocol** and is the protocol used to request and deliver web pages.

This protocol operates over IP. IP is the protocol used between routers and devices. HTTP is an end-to-end protocol between the PC and the web server. In computing, protocols often operate in layers. Imagine the process of sending a letter to a friend. The Post Office operates the lower level protocol between towns to physically deliver your letter (like IP between the routers and LANs). The letter is the higher level protocol that communicates end-to-end between you and your friend (like HTTP requesting a page from a web server and the server sending the page back). See diagram over the page.

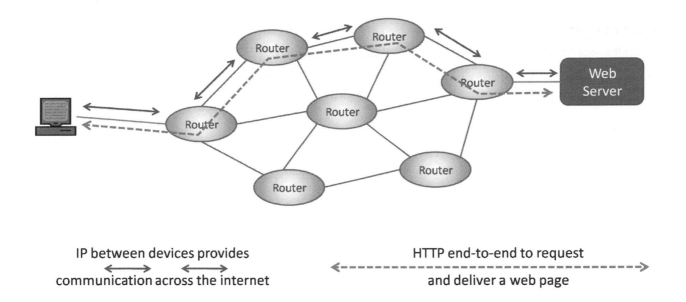

IP between devices provides
⟷   ⟷
communication across the internet

HTTP end-to-end to request
⟵ - ⟶
and deliver a web page

Connecting to the Internet

The OCR Specification says that you should be able to:

- describe the hardware needed to connect to the internet including modems, routers etc

There are many ways to connect to the internet:

- **Modem:**

  This is the cheapest but slowest type of connection, only 56kb/s. It uses the telephone network to create a connection from your computer to the internet. Your computer and the internet are both **digital**, designed for computer traffic. The telephone network is **analogue**, designed for voice traffic. The modem is a device that converts the digital signal from the computer into an analogue signal, and vice versa at the other end. As well as being slow, this method means that you can only use the phone line for one transmission at a time; if you're on the internet then the phone cannot be used at the same time.

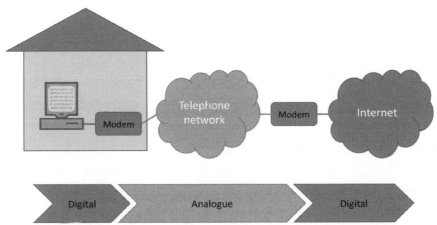

- **Local router:**

  Very few home PCs are connected to the internet using a modem these days. Many of us will have more than one computer at home and will have a wireless router somewhere in the house. The computers all connect to the router to get an internet connection and can also communicate with each other as they now form a small LAN.

  The router can be connected to the internet using:

  - The fibre optic cable that delivers your cable TV service
  - The part of the phone line that connects your house to the local exchange using **broadband** technology. This is not the same as using a modem to transmit over the telephone network itself, but is just using the local cable. It is digital transmission all the way and allows the use of the computers and phone line at the same time, unlike a modem.

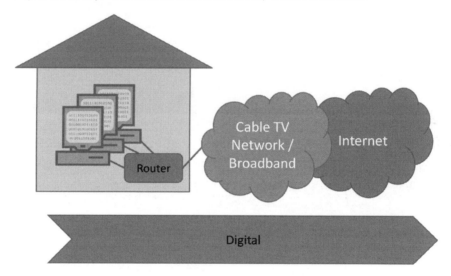

Broadband and cable TV services offer speeds in excess of 2Mb/s and in places services up to 24Mb/s are being advertised (Oct 2011). The modem running at 56kb/s is just 0.05Mb/s (56/1024 to convert kilobits per second into megabits per second).

If your computer is connected to a LAN then there will be an internet connection provided from a router connected to the LAN. The principal is the same as a home router but it will be a more powerful router.

CREATING WEB PAGES IN HTML

The OCR Specification says that you should be able to:

- explain the importance of HTML and its derivatives as a standard for the creation of web pages

Web pages are written in a programming language called **HTML**, HyperText Markup Language. HTML is used to describe the page content. It is used with a Cascading Style Sheet (**CSS**) that defines how the content is styled. Some styling can be coded with HTML but it is considered good practise to use CSS for styling and HTML for content.

!!! See HTML and CSS in action...

Check out this website to see how the same HTML content can look with different Cascading Style Sheets!

www.csszengarden.com

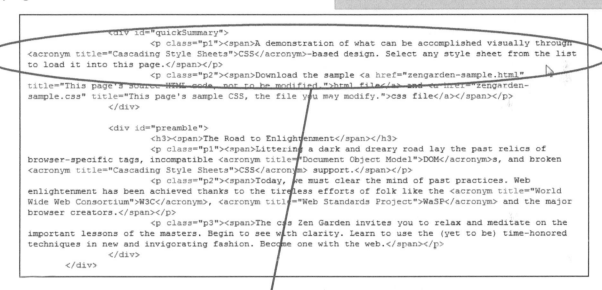

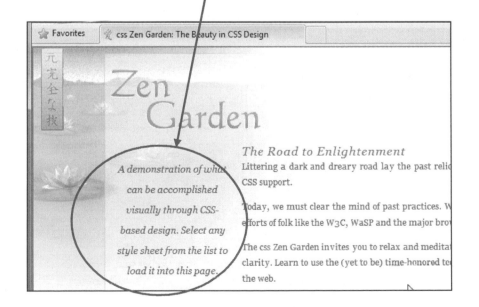

HTML is coded using **tags** that define the page structure. You can write HTML in a basic text editor and save the file as "filename.html". You can then run the page in your browser. Here is a very basic webpage in HTML:

```
<html>
  <head>
    <title>My first web page</title>
  </head>
  <body>
    <h1> Susan Robson </h1>
    <h2> Where I'm From </h2>
    <p> I grew up in Crowborough in East Sussex.  It's a large village just
        North of Brighton. </p>
    <h2> What I like </h2>
    <p> I  like  walking,  cycling  and  skiing.  I  also  like  shoes,
        chocolate cake and penguins.</p>
    <p>More  on  <a  href=http://www.kidzone.ws/animals/penguins/index.htm  >
        penguins!</a>
    <img src="penguin.jpg" width=80 height=60>  </p>
  </body>
</html>
```

Tag	What it does
\<head> \</head>	Start and end tags for information <u>about</u> this page, not text that appears on the page.
\<title> \</title>	The text between these tags appears in the blue bar at the top of the browser window.
\<body> \</body>	The HTML between the body tags defines the page content.
\<p> \</p>	Paragraph tags that start and end a paragraph.
\<h1> \</h1> **\<h2> \</h2>**	Heading tags will go either end of heading text. The CSS will define how these look but normally heading text is bigger than normal page text.
\<img src.....>	The image source tag references a picture file and defines basic parameters such as size.
\<a href...>	An href tag is a hyperlink reference that the following text will be linked to.

The web page it produces look like this:

When you create a page using HTML it is not a website that other people can get to yet; you can only see the page in your browser because you have access to the file. A website must be published to the internet so other people can access it. This can be done by uploading it to your own web server or you can upload it to someone else's web server. If you use someone else's server this is called "hosting". Internet Service Providers (ISPs) offer this as a service, sometime free for small sites if you are already a customer.

Writing a website using HTML would be time- consuming so there are application packages available to help design a website and create the HTML code for you. One example of this is Dreamweaver.

!!! **Useful website...**

An excellent site for details on HTML code is: www.htmldog.com

SECURITY

The OCR Specification says that you should be able to:

- explain the need for security measures in networks, such as user access levels, suitable passwords and encryption techniques
- describe and justify network policies such as acceptable use, disaster recovery, failover, backup, archiving

Security is about keeping your computer and the files stored on it safe from hazards. These hazards come in the form of viruses, hackers, hardware failures, software faults and natural disasters such as floods and fires, but the biggest hazard to networked computers with shared resources is other users!

Network security measures cover three important areas:

1. Preventive measures	Aimed at stopping a hazardous event from occurring	• Access rights • Firewalls • Physical security such as locking rooms • Passwords • Encryption • Acceptable use policy
2. Detective measures	Aimed at detecting when data has been corrupted or systems have been compromised	• Virus checking software • Firewall software • Fire alarms • Audit trails
3. Corrective measures	Aimed at correcting or restoring the system after problems have occurred	• Backup & restore procedures • Redundant hardware / Failover • Disaster recovery procedures

Chapter 4, "Software" talks about security software for a standalone computer. The anti-virus software, firewall and spyware protection software are all equally applicable in a network.

Security Precautions

- **Access Rights:**

User access rights should be set for disks, folders and files so users can only access what they need to. At school you can probably read files on a shared area but not edit them; this is Read-Only access. The teacher will have Read-Write access to these folders. Some folders you won't even be able to see.

In a work environment, the Accounts staff will have access to payroll details but other departments will not. The Data Protection Act says that employers must keep personal data secure so setting appropriate access rights is a legal responsibility as well as a good idea.

- **Encryption**

There are devices that can read network transmissions from the cables just by scanning the emissions; they don't even have to be plugged into the network. Also anything transmitted over a network can be intercepted and read. This takes place without leaving any trace so nobody would know that it had happened.

One way of stopping this unauthorised access to data is to encrypt anything sent on a network. Encryption changes the data before it is transmitted so it can only be deciphered by someone with the appropriate key. To anyone intercepting the message it would be unintelligible.

When you buy something on the internet or use internet banking you may have noticed that instead of HTTP in front of the domain name it changes to HTTPS. It works in the same way as HTTP but is encrypted so your payment details are kept secure.

- **Password Protection**

In a networked environment such as a school or a company, many of the computers are used by more than one person. Even if employees have their own computer it may be in an open plan office. The easiest way to stop unauthorised access to your computer or your files is to use a combination of username and password.

The password should never be shared with friends or stuck on a post-it note under the keyboard (yes, people really do!). Also, the password should be "strong". This means that it is not easy to guess, it probably contains letters, numbers and symbols and is at least 6 characters long. Some companies make employees change their password every month but this doesn't really work because people usually just add the month number on the end because it is easy to remember.

For additional security against people trying lots of different passwords to get into someone else's account, the account can be locked after a certain number of failed attempts.

Network Policies

As well as configuration and software precautions there are procedural precautions a company can take to protect its data. These procedures and policies include:

- **Backup & Restore Procedures**

The staff that manage a network will backup the servers regularly. A backup is a copy of all the users' files, which can be restored in the event of files getting corrupted or deleted. Backup copies must be made regularly; how often will depend on the nature of the system to a certain extent. In some businesses a daily backup may be sufficient but in another business files may be backed up every hour or weekly. Backups are normally made using a removal hard disk or cassette tape. The medium has to be high capacity and portable so it can be stored in a fire-proof safe or off site.

- **Archiving**

Often there is a large amount of data stored on a computer system that is no longer needed on a regular basis. However, you cannot delete it just in case it is needed again or because a company is legally required to keep some records for a number of years (for example tax returns). Archiving is when the data is taken off the main system and stored, usually on magnetic tape as it is cheap. It can be loaded back onto the system if it is needed again. It is not a copy like a backup. The point is to free up space on the main computer system.

- **Disaster Recovery**

Some companies would not be able to operate at all if their computer systems went down.   These companies will have a **disaster recovery plan** that would enable them to keep on doing business even in the event of something catastrophic happening. Catastrophic events that destroy a whole building and all of the servers include things like fire, a tidal wave or a bomb.

Data backup goes offsite to a disaster recovery company

A disaster recovery plan includes the ability to replicate the computer system in a very short time. This would involve:

- o   Data being backed up regularly
- o   Duplicate hardware systems being available very quickly
- o   The backup data being restored on the new hardware so the company could carry on as normal

Companies can either buy their own redundant hardware just in case but they are more likely to pay a disaster recovery company for the service. There are companies that specialise in providing hardware at short notice to companies.

- **Failover**

When a computer system is mission-critical to a company it cannot be offline at all. Obviously hardware failures still happen but when they do the computer system will swap over to a spare component straight away. Spare components built into a computer system for this purpose are referred to as **redundant**.

A system that has lots of redundancy built into it is described as **fault-tolerant** because when faults happen the system copes with it.   **Failover** is the process of swapping to the spare/redundant component. Failover happens automatically and transparently (without the user noticing).

- **Acceptable Use Policy**

When you started at your school you probably had to sign an Acceptable Use Policy before you were given a username and password. This policy probably said you must not use other people's accounts, access pornography, play games or do anything else that is not related to doing your school work.

Employees will all sign a similar agreement. This is a contract between you and the school/company saying you agree to only use the network for certain things. In school you probably get away with playing games now and then but at work a company can sack you for going against the agreement you signed.

The Acceptable Use Policy makes it clear to all network users what is acceptable and what is not.

Hazard	Security Precaution
Accidental data deletion/corruption by users.	Backup & restore procedures
Unauthorised access to files/folders by employees	Passwords, firewall, access rights Acceptable use policy
Hardware failure or software faults	Backup & restore procedures Failover
Hackers	Passwords, firewall, access rights
Natural disasters: fire, flood, lightening strike etc	Backup & restore procedures Disaster recovery
Bomb	Backup & restore procedures Disaster recovery
Curious computing students "just seeing what happens when you click..."!!	Access rights Backup & restore Acceptable use policy (!)

FILE TYPES AND FILE COMPRESSION

The OCR Specification says that you should be able to:

- explain the importance of compressing files that are transmitted via the internet
- describe the differences between lossy and lossless compression
- describe common file standards associated with the internet such as JPG, GIF, PDF, MP3, MPEG

When data is transmitted across the internet it will go through many different physical links between routers. The connection from a computer or a LAN into the internet is likely to be the slowest part of this route, as you probably know from experience. At home you may have quite a slow network connection and it may take a while for web pages to load.

One way of speeding up how quickly files can be transmitted across the internet is to compress them to make them smaller. Smaller files take less time to transmit over a network.

Understanding how compression affects files is important as the type of compression selected will affect how the image looks or the audio track sounds. The final use of the file will dictate how much you can compress the files and still have a file that is useable.

Compression can be considered in two categories:

- **Lossy compression:** a data encoding method where files are compressed by removing some of the detail. For example, photographs can be stored using fewer colours so fewer bits are needed per pixel (see Chapter 2, "Data Representation"). Lossy compression is used to compress multimedia data such as picture, audio files and video files.
- **Lossless compression:** a data encoding method where files are compressed but no data is lost. Essential for text and data files. For example, bank records must keep all of the data; you cannot transmit a bank statement and miss out a few zeros because they don't matter too much!

Still Image File Types

Still images are photographs and vector graphics (such as clipart). As we saw in Chapter 2, "Data Representation", the way we store images will affect the size. The colour depth is one factor. If you use 8 bits to represent each pixel then you can use up to 256 different colours in the picture. "Truecolor" is the name given to a picture representation using 24 bits per pixel where the colours are a mix of Red, Green and Blue (RGB).

To compress and image you can use fewer bits per pixel. A bitmap image (.bmp) or .png file is a lossless version of the picture. If you save the same photograph as a JPEG file then it is still a high quality image with a colour depth of 24 bits but some of the data is lost where it is unlikely to be noticed. Digital cameras mostly store pictures as JPEG files. If you save the same picture as a GIF file then you make the file much smaller as you only use 8 bits per pixel instead of 24 bits per pixel. The human eye can tell the difference at this stage. You will see solid blocks of colour instead of gradual transitions in the photograph. However, for small pictures on websites that will only be viewed as a thumbnail, GIF files are fine and take less time to load on a webpage.

Here is a section of a photograph blown up so you can see the difference:

JPEG version: *GIF version:*

Video File Types

Video files are mostly stored as MPEG format. There are two versions for different quality requirements though: MPEG-1 is great for low resolution sequences on a website but if you want high resolution full-screen video then you need MPEG-2.

Audio File Types

Audio files can also be compressed. The demand for music downloads drove the need for a better compression method and MP3 became the dominant compression type. We can download MP3 files from the internet very quickly and their size means that we can store hundreds of tracks on an MP3 player. Most people cannot tell the difference in quality between an MP3 track and a track from a CD. You can get about 120 tracks on a CD if they are in MP3 format though.

Document File Types

You can create documents in any word processing or desk-top publishing package. Each package will have its own file format. For example, if you create a document in Microsoft Word it will be saved as a .docx file. This is fine when we are working on our own documents but when we are sharing documents across the internet this format might not suit everyone.

PDF (Portable Document Format) is an open file format, capable of displaying a document on any hardware or any operating system. This means that PDF files can be downloaded from websites anywhere in the world and read on a Windows PC, Apple Mac, tablet, book reader, smart phone or whatever the latest gadget is.

When a PDF document is created it captures all the elements of a printed page as an electronic image that you can view, navigate, print or forward to someone else. When the PDF file is created you can also set options that allow the reader to use copy & paste or block this feature.

Word processing packages and desk-top publishers will all be able to write PDF files as well as their own format (picture shown is from Microsoft Word 2007). The device on which the document is read will need PDF reader software, which is freely available and already installed on many devices.

PDF files are not compressed but you can use a lossless compression algorithm such as ZIP to reduce their size.

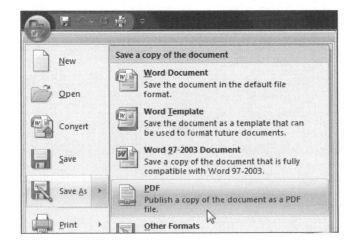

Summary of File Types

Type	File suffix	Compression Type	Explanation
Bitmap	.bmp	-	Uncompressed still image file
Portable Network Graphic	.png	Lossless	Colour depth = 24 bits, RGB, 16.7 million different colours
JPEG	.jpg	Lossy	Good for photographs. Colour depth = 24 bits, RGB, 16.7 million different colours
Graphic Interchange Format	.gif	Lossless	Colour depth = 8 bits (only 256 colours) Good for images with large areas of solid colour Ideal for web graphics Although this is a lossless compression, images with higher colour depths are often converted into GIFs to make them smaller (this process is called "quantisation" but is not in the GCSE specification!)
QuickTime	.mov	Lossless	Audio files
Windows Media Player	.wmv .wav	Lossy	Audio files: Files are not as small as MP3
MP3	.mp3	Lossy	Audio files: Designed for downloading music from the internet. In MP3 format you could fit 120 songs on a CD.
MPEG -1	.mpg	Lossy	Video files: Suitable for small low-resolution sequences on CD
MPEG-2	.mp2	Lossy	Video files: Suitable for full-screen, high resolution video on DVD
Portable Document Format	.pdf	-	An uncompressed document format that is universally accessible.

GLOSSARY OF TERMS

Networking

LAN	A collection of computers and peripheral devices connected together within a single site.
WAN	A collection of computers and LANs connected together over a geographically-remote area, using leased infrastructure.
Topology	A description of how devices are connected together. Does not necessarily represent physical layout.
Bus	A topology where each device is connected to a main cable, referred to as the bus. Any device can transmit at any time but only one transmission can occur on the main bus at any one time.
Ring	A topology where each device is connected to the next in a loop. Uses a token-passing protocol to manage transmission by one device at a time.
Star	A topology where each device has its own cable connecting it to a central device, which can be a switch or a server.
Peer-to-peer	A method of organising devices in a network where devices are all of equal status rather than having specialised roles. Each computer can access resources on another computer, assuming access rights have been granted by the other computer.
Client-server	A method of organising devices in a network where some computers have specialised roles: servers. The servers provide resources and services to the other computers, known as clients. Management of the network and shared resources/files is centralised at the server.
Hub	A hardware device that provides connectivity onto a LAN cable. A multiport box that has a connection to the LAN from one side and several computers on the other. Can be wireless or cabled.
Switch	A hardware device that is similar to a hub but it has built-in intelligence. Computers connected to a Switch form a star topology LAN.
Wireless Access Point	The device to which a computer connects wirelessly. Can be a wireless hub or a wireless switch.
NIC	Network Interface Card: the card that goes in a computer to provide a connection to a LAN. Can be wireless or cabled.

Networking (continued)

MAC address	A unique hardware number allocated to every NIC. It is a 48-bit address, usually written in hex, eg: `00-09-7C-F1-F7-85`
Message	A communication between devices. Split into packets for sending over a network and put back together again at the other end.
Packet	A fixed size chunk of a message created to send a message over a network. It has its own header containing data such as the destination address and packet number (so the message can be put back together in the right order).
Protocol	A set of rules that defines how devices communicate. Eg: IP, HTTP, HTTPS

Internet

Internet	A worldwide network where computers and networks in geographically separate locations are connected together using a variety of communication links. Devices communicate using Internet Protocol (IP).
Routers	The hardware devices that make up the backbone of the internet as well as (smaller ones) providing connectivity from a LAN to the internet. Use Internet Protocol to communicate with each other.
Modem	The hardware device used to convert the digital transmission from a computer into an analogue signal that can be carried over the analogue telephone network. A method of accessing the internet.
Digital	A transmission signal that is made up of separate values (numbers), as opposed to the continuously changing signal in analogue transmissions.
Analogue	A transmission signal that is continuously changing, as opposed to being made up of separate values (numbers). Sound in the real world is analogue.
Broadband	A method of connecting to the internet using the site's normal phone line to carry digital transmissions. Allows more than one device (phone and computer) to share the link.
WWW	World-Wide Web: a collection of pages distributed on servers connected to the internet. Uses HTTP to request and send pages to browsers.
HTTP	HyperText Transfer Protocol: the protocol used by a browser to send page requests to a server and also by the server to send back the required page.
HTTPS	A secure version of HTTP where transmissions are encrypted.

Internet (continued)

IP addressing	A method of labeling any device connected to the network with a unique numerical value. Uses four bytes usually expressed in this notation: 123.123.003.243
Domain name	The text label for a website in the internet: www.bbc.co.uk It corresponds to an IP address for that site.
DNS servers	Domain Name System server: a database of domain names and associated IP addresses stored on servers. There are many DNS servers distributed across the internet, which communicate with each other.
HTML	HyperText Markup Language: the programming language used to define the layout and content of a webpage. Uses tags in conjunction with a CSS to control how content is displayed.
CSS	Cascading Style Sheet: defines the formatting and layout of the content defined by the HTML code. Eg: `<H1>` may be 32pt Arial in Green.
Tags	Labels that go around the content (text, pictures etc) to define what they will look like on the page. Eg: `<H1> A heading </H1>`

Security

User Access Levels	A network policy that defines which users can see which folders and files and the type of access they have to them. Eg: Read-Only or Read-Write.
Encryption	Where the data is changed, using a key, before it is transmitted so that it can only be deciphered by another device with the appropriate key. To anyone intercepting the message it would be unintelligible.
Acceptable Use Policy	An agreement that computer users will sign/agree to before being allowed access to a computer or the network.
Failover	When a hardware component fails, the computer switches over to a redundant component without the service to the user being interrupted.
Redundant	Spare, ready to be used if another component fails. Relates to spare hardware components in fault-tolerant systems that use failover.
Fault-Tolerant	A system that has been designed to cope with hardware failures. Uses redundant hardware and failover usually.
Backup	A copy of data is taken from a live computer system as a precaution against system failure or corruption/deletion of individual files/folders. To be restored in the event of data loss.

Security (continued)

Archiving	Files are removed from the main computer system but kept in long-term storage, just in case they are needed in the future or because the law requires they be kept. Creates space on main system.
Disaster Recovery	A collection of precautions that ensures the computer system can be reestablished very quickly after a catastrophe. Includes backup policy, complete hardware system available offsite at short notice and policies to restore data and applications on the replacement hardware.

Compression

Compression	Making files smaller for quicker transmission over a network.
Lossless compression	File is compressed with no loss of essential data.
Lossy compression	Files are compressed by removing some data that is less essential for the purpose. For example, using fewer colours in a picture (reduce colour depth).

PAST EXAM QUESTIONS & EXAMPLE ANSWERS

From the specimen paper

2   A classroom in a primary school has 6 stand alone computers. The school decides to connect them to form a LAN.

(a)   What is a LAN?

Local Area Network, a collection of computers and peripheral devices connected together within a single site.   [1]

(b)   State two advantages of connecting the computers into a LAN.

Advantage 1

Resources can be shared eg: files, printers, scanners

Advantage 2

Communication: users can communicate using email and messaging   [2]

(c)   The school decides to use the star topology to create the LAN.

Describe what is meant by a star topology. You may use a diagram.

All computers are connected to a central server or switch.

Each computer has its own cable to the central computer

Shared resources on the central computer eg: files and printer

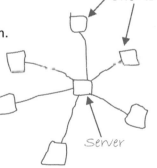

[2]

(d)   State two additional hardware items which will be needed to create the LAN. For each, state why it is needed.

Item 1   *Network Interface Card*

Reason why needed   *It provides a port on the computer to connect a network cable to*

Item 2   *Server*

Reason why needed   *It provides network services to the client computers such as storing shared folders and files*   [4]

From Jan 2011 Paper

2 A small business has three stand-alone computers, a printer and an internet connection in an office.

(a) State two advantages of connecting the computers to create a local area network.

1. *So users on the individual computers can share files rather than having duplicate copies*

2. *So staff can communicate using email*   [2]

(b) Describe, using a diagram, how the computers can be connected to each other using a bus topology, stating what hardware will be needed.

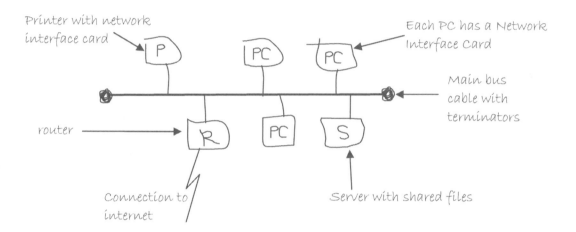

[6]

CHAPTER 7:   PROGRAMMING

As part of this GCSE you will have learnt a **high level programming language** such as Pascal, Delphi or Visual Basic. This topic is all about designing **algorithms**, writing code using best practice and testing the programs to make sure they meet the requirements.

In the A453 unit you will do a controlled assessment programming task, which will use this programming knowledge in a very practical way.

In the A451 theory unit will also be examined on your understanding of algorithms, coding and testing.

This chapter does not teach you how to program in a specific programming language but addresses the theory you will need to understand for the A451 exam.

ALGORITHMS

The OCR Specification says that you should be able to:

*   understand algorithms (written in pseudocode or flow diagram), explain what they do, and correct or complete them
*   produce algorithms in pseudocode or flow diagrams to solve problems

In computing we write programs or create computer systems to "solve a problem". The **problem** is the need or requirement we have to meet. The solution could be a simple program but is more likely to be a complex suite of hardware and software in a real-world scenario.

Understanding how to solve the problem is important. You cannot just start coding at line 1 and hope to get a working solution straight away.

The outline of the solution is called an **algorithm**. Algorithm is defined as: a series of steps to solve a problem. Algorithms can be expressed in several ways. This chapter will look at creating an outline algorithm with a **system flow chart** and then creating a more detailed algorithm from this using **pseudocode**.

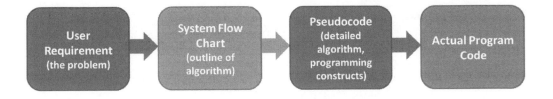

System Flow Charts

A system flow chart is an industry-standard design tool, which is used to show an algorithm diagrammatically. There are standard symbols that you will need to understand:

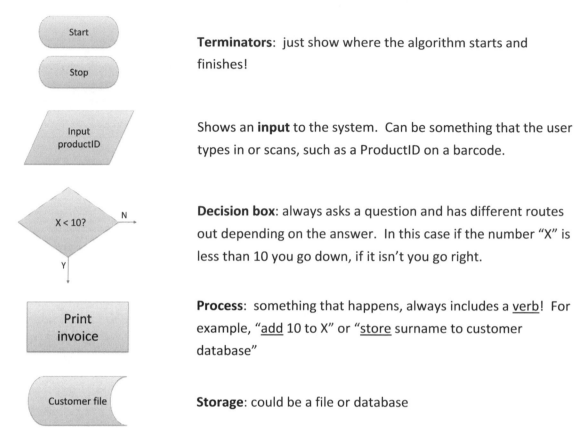

Terminators: just show where the algorithm starts and finishes!

Shows an **input** to the system. Can be something that the user types in or scans, such as a ProductID on a barcode.

Decision box: always asks a question and has different routes out depending on the answer. In this case if the number "X" is less than 10 you go down, if it isn't you go right.

Process: something that happens, always includes a <u>verb</u>! For example, "<u>add</u> 10 to X" or "<u>store</u> surname to customer database"

Storage: could be a file or database

This very simple example shows the algorithm for taking a pizza order. The program must get the pizza size first and then get one or more toppings.

Notice the following:

- There is a loop to get more than one topping. This loop is controlled by the decision box that asks, "Enough toppings?". If the answer is "Yes" to this question the program stops, otherwise it keeps asking for the next topping.

- The line that loops around joins the middle of a line, it does not come into a box.

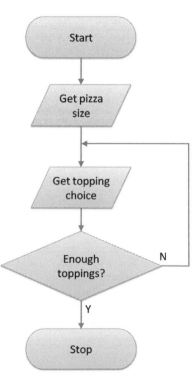

Here is a more complex system requirement. The problem is as follows:

- A computerised form prompts a user to enter their email address.

- The validation rules check if the address has an @ symbol in it. If it doesn't, an error message is displayed, the text box is cleared and the system asks the user to enter the email address again. This continues until an appropriate address is entered.

- The system then checks that the email address has been typed in lowercase, if not it converts it to lowercase.

- Once the email address is ok it is stored in the customer database.

The System Flow Chart for this could be as follows:

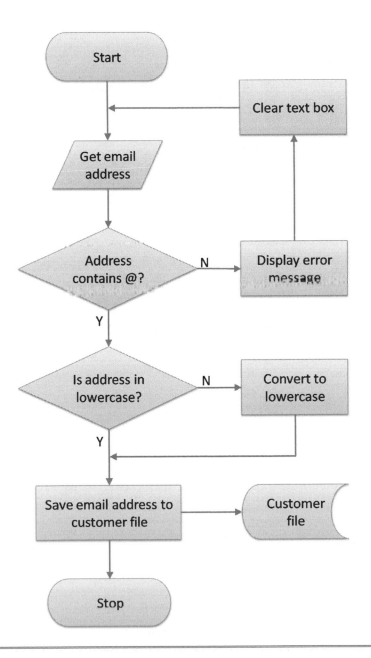

Pseudocode

Pseudocode is when we write an algorithm in programming-style constructs but not in an actual programming language. You do not need to worry about the detailed syntax or be precise about how the code will do something, just capture the steps you will need in your program. As we said before, an algorithm is a series of steps to solve a problem so that is all you are doing at this stage.

Once you have fairly detailed pseudocode you can use it as comments in your program and write the actual code under each step!

CONTROL FLOW IN IMPERATIVE LANGUAGES

The OCR Specification says that you should be able to:

- understand and use sequence in an algorithm
- understand and use selection in an algorithm (IF and CASE statements)
- understand and use iteration in an algorithm (FOR, WHILE and REPEAT loops)

There are three pseudocode constructs used to write algorithms (and in actual code):

Sequence

Sequence is just a matter of writing the steps down in the order they need to happen. For example:

```
Get the product price
Get the quantity
Total = quantity x price
Output "Total price is " + total
```

Selection

There are two basic selection constructs that you will learn when you program. IF…THEN…ELSE allows you to choose between two options. By nesting these or having several in a row you can choose between several options but this is more efficiently achieved by the CASE statement. Both constructs are shown below showing the key words in bold:

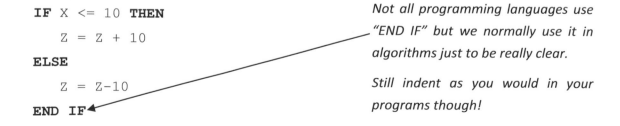

```
IF X <= 10 THEN
    Z = Z + 10
ELSE
    Z = Z-10
END IF
```

Not all programming languages use "END IF" but we normally use it in algorithms just to be really clear.

Still indent as you would in your programs though!

The following selections show three different ways of coding a menu system where the user can choose between three options:

Method 1: Using multiple IF statements:

```
IF MenuChoice=1 THEN
    Do this thing
END IF

IF MenuChoice=2 THEN
    Do the other thing
END IF

IF MenuChoice=3 THEN
    Self-destruct
END IF
```

These are three separate IF...THEN statements so the computer will have to execute the second and third IF statements, even if the user selected '1' from the menu.

This is not efficient coding but it will work.

Method 2: Using multiple **nested** IF statements:

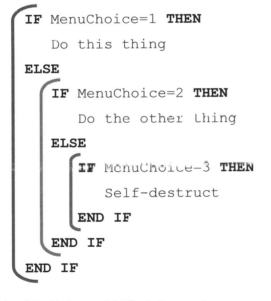

```
IF MenuChoice=1 THEN
    Do this thing
ELSE
    IF MenuChoice=2 THEN
        Do the other thing
    ELSE
        IF MenuChoice-3 THEN
            Self-destruct
        END IF
    END IF
END IF
```

This still uses three separate IF...THEN statements but they are nested so that the computer will only execute the IF statement tests until it finds one that is true.

This is more efficient than method 1 but for several choices it is difficult for a programmer to follow.

Method 3: Using a CASE statement:

```
CASE MenuChoice OF
    1:  Do this thing
    2:  Do the other thing
    3:  Self-destruct
ELSE
    Write "You must choose 1 -3!"
END CASE
```

The CASE statement is designed for coding multiple choices in a program, such as a menu of 3 options where the user will enter one choice.

Can you see how much clearer this chunk of code is than the nested-IF version above?

Iteration

There are three basic iteration (loop) constructs that you will learn when you program.

The **FOR** loop allows you to execute a group of steps 1 or more times, for a specific number of times.

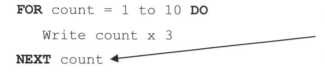

```
FOR count = 1 to 10 DO
    Write count x 3
NEXT count
```

*Not all programming languages use "**next nnn**" but we normally use it in algorithms just to be really clear that count is incremented each time around the loop.*

A **REPEAT** loop is controlled by a condition <u>at the end</u> of the loop. It will, therefore, always execute the following steps <u>at least once</u>. Here is an example of an algorithm that uses a REPEAT loop:

```
Count = 1
REPEAT
    Write count x 3
    Count = count + 1
UNTIL count = 10
```

A **WHILE** loop is controlled by a condition <u>at the start</u> of the loop. It will, therefore, execute the following steps <u>zero or more</u> times. This is important when you read from a file, for example, when you need to check if the file is empty <u>before</u> you try to read from it. Here is an example of an algorithm that uses a WHILE loop:

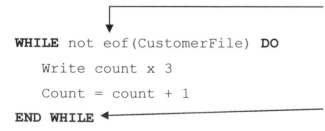

```
WHILE not eof(CustomerFile) DO
    Write count x 3
    Count = count + 1
END WHILE
```

eof means End Of File!
eof(CustomerFile) checks if the file pointer is at the end of the file called CustomerFile.

Not all programming languages use "end while" but we normally use it in algorithms to be clear where the loop ends.

> **‼️ NB...**
>
> A **condition** is a **boolean expression** that will be true or false at a particular point in the program. Conditions are used to control iteration and selection statements.

If we convert the system flow chart from the previous section into pseudocode it would look something like this:

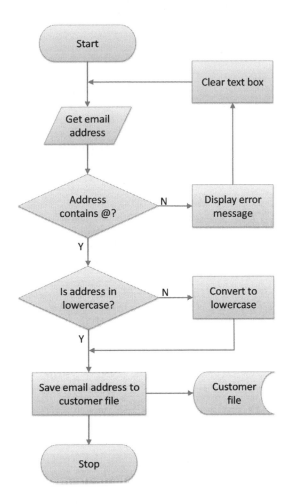

```
REPEAT
    Get EmailAddreess
    IF EmailAddress contains @ THEN
        HasAtSign = true
    ELSE
        HasAtSign - False
        Display error message
        Clear text box
    END IF
UNTIL HasAtSign



IF EmailAddress is not lowercase THEN
    Convert to lowercase
END IF



Open customer file
Find customer record
Write EmailAddress to file
Close Customer file


END of Program
```

In pseudocode you can use phrases like, "`IF EmailAddress contains @ THEN`". At this stage a general statement is fine. When you write the actual code you will need to use the appropriate string handling function, for example:

$$AtPosition:=InString(variable,'@')$$

Notice that the pseudocode is indented like a real program. This is good practice and makes your algorithm easier to follow. Also, get into the habit of naming items without spaces. For example, here we've used "`EmailAddress`". The **PascalCase** format (all words capitalised but no spaces) makes it easy to read and means you don't need to use spaces or underscores. You cannot use spaces in identifiers in any programming language so don't use them in your design.

> ??? **For you to find out...**
>
> Investigate PascalCase, CamelCase and Hungarian notation. Which of these did you use in the database unit when you named components on your forms?

PROGRAMMING LANGUAGES

> The OCR Specification says that you should be able to:
>
> - explain the difference between high level code and machine code
> - explain the need for translators to convert high level code to machine code
> - describe the characteristics of an assembler, a compiler and an interpreter

In Chapter 2, "Data Representation", we looked at how computers store instructions and data as binary. Program code in binary is referred to as **machine code** and is known as the first generation of programming languages.

To write code at the processor level we use **assembly language**, which is also known as second generation language. There are lots of different assembly languages; one for every different processor architecture. The code is written in **mnemonics**, abbreviated text commands such as LOAD, STORE, ADD.

Human beings find it easier to write programs in languages that are suited to the type of problem and languages that look more like normal languages. 3rd generation languages were invented for this, otherwise known as **high level languages**. There are lots of different programming languages to suit different types of problem. For example, you might use Delphi to write a forms-based data processing application but you would use Java to code web-based applets.

Independent of hardware (portable)	3rd Generation	High Level Languages (HLL)	In statements:
			
			`Rate:=3.02`
			`Used:=5672`
			`BillAmount:=Rate*Used`

Language is processor specific	2nd Generation	Assembly Language	In mnemonics:
			
			`LOAD #34`
			`ADD &4F3A`
			`STORE &39FC`

	1st Generation	Machine Code	In binary:
			
			`1010100011010101`
			`0100100101010101`

Hardware

Comparing High Level Languages & Machine Code

Features of the two types of languages compare as follows:

Machine Code	High Level Languages
Processor specific: one instruction set per processor architecture, won't work on another machine	Portable: will work on different types of machine/processor
Designed with hardware in mind	Designed with a type of problem in mind
Machine code operations relate directly to an assembly language command; one-to-one relationship	One high level program instruction will be translated into several machine code instructions

Translating programs into Machine Code

Whatever language a program is written in, it must be translated into machine code so it can run on the processor. Translators are a type of **system software** (see chapter 4, "Software"). There are three types of **translator** programs that do this:

- **Assemblers:**
  Convert assembly language into machine code. A simple conversion as every assembly language instruction is translated into a single machine code instruction.

- **Compilers and Interpreters:**
  Convert a high level programming language into machine code. This is a more complex translation as a single instruction in Delphi, for example, can result in many machine code instructions.

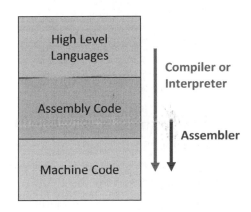

A compiler translates a high level programming language into machine code. The machine code version is then run by the computer. This compiled version doesn't need the original **source code** or the compiler in order to run. When you buy commercial software you are buying an executable version, what we call **object code**.

The benefit of using a compiler is that object code can be distributed to customers easily, without giving them your valuable source code! If you distributed source code there market could be flooded with rip-off versions within days. (Some people are happy to share their code and deliberately release their software as Open Source, see Chapter 4, "Software").

The disadvantage is that any software problems that occur in the object code version are harder to diagnose.

An interpreter is an alternative way of translating high level programs. It only translates and executes one line at a time so it doesn't need the same amount of memory as the compiler, which uses a lot of memory. The interpreter is often used when software is being developed as it is easy to pin-point where a problem is in the code.

The disadvantage of interpretation is the speed. Programs run much slower as every line has to be translated first. There is no object code created, the interpreter translates the program every time it is run. Also, if you have a loop where instructions are executed several times, the interpreter will translate them from scratch every time around the loop!

The table below compares compilers and interpreters:

Compiler	Interpreter
Translates the whole program to produce the executable object code.	Translates and executes one line at a time.
The object code is the version that the computer runs.	The source code is the version that the computer runs.
Faster run time because the program is translated once, object code is run after that.	Slower run time because the program is translated every time it is run.
Customers cannot see the actual code you wrote when you distribute the program.	If you distributed source code with an interpreter then customers would have your actual code.
Used for distributed software.	Used in development.

HANDLING DATA IN ALGORITHMS

The OCR Specification says that you should be able to:

- define the terms variable and constant as used in an imperative language
- use variables and constants
- describe the data types integer, real, Boolean, character and string
- select and justify appropriate data types for a given program

Constants

In a program there are certain values that remain the same (constant) while the program runs. The programmer could use the actual number in the code each time but it is considered good practice to give the number a unique name (an **identifier**) and then use that name throughout the program. We declare **constants** at the start of our programs and then refer to them as needed in the code. For example:

At the start of the program: `CONST`
                               `VATRate = 0.175;`

Later in the program code: `SellPrice:=NetPrice*VATRate+NetPrice;`

Please note though, this does not mean that the constant's value will never change during the lifetime of the system! For example, the VAT rate will stay the same (constant) while the program runs in the shop each day but, after the next budget, it may change. The value allocated to that constant will then need to be edited in the program.

The two main benefits of declaring a constant are:

- When its value changes, you only have to edit it in one place rather than looking for every place in the program where you used that number.

- The code will be easier to read and understand because the constant's identifier will be used instead of a number. This makes your code easier to debug and, later on, maintain.

Variables & Data Types

When a program runs it processes data, which must be stored in memory while the program is running. We need to name these locations so we can refer to them in the program. As the program runs the values in these locations might change so they are called **variables**. For example: a variable called "total" might change several times as many numbers are added to it or a variable called "surname" will change as the program processes a list of customer orders.

Each variable has an **identifier** (unique name) that refers to a location in memory where the data item will be stored. Each variable also has a **data type** that defines:

- the type of data that will be stored at the memory location and therefore the operations that can be performed on this data item (described later in this chapter)
- how much space will be needed for that data item.

We declare variables at the start of a program so when the program runs, the appropriate memory can be reserved to store the data. The following is an example from a Pascal/Delphi program:

```
Var
    num1, num2   :integer;
    total        :real;
    choice       :char;
    username     :string;
    found        :Boolean;
```

The word "var" tells the computer that variable declarations follow. The word to the left of the colon is the variable's identifiers/names. The word to the right of the colon is the **data type** (see below).

The table below shows a list of data types and the typical amount of memory that each would need. Note that the amount varies for different programming languages so an integer may need 2 bytes in one language but 4 bytes in another.

Data Type	Type of Data	Typical Amount of Memory
Integer	A whole number, such as 3, 45,-453	2 bytes
Real	A number with a fractional part such as 34.456, -9.234	4 bytes
Char	A single character, where a character can be any letter, digit, punctuation mark or symbol that can be typed.	1 byte
String	Zero or more characters. A string can be null (empty), just one character or several characters. Most programming languages have a limit of 255 characters if the programmer does not specify the maximum size.	Up to 255 bytes (1 byte per character in the string)
Boolean	A boolean variable has the value True or False.	1 byte

Operations on common data types

> The OCR Specification says that you should be able to:
>
> - perform common operations on numeric and Boolean data

Operations are things you can do to specific types of data. For example, you can perform arithmetic operations on numbers and you can perform string handling operations on text.

Numerical Data Types:

Operations that can be performed on numerical data types are as follows:

Arithmetic operations

(give a numerical result)

eg: 25 + 3 = 28

- + (addition)
- - (subtraction)
- * (multiplication)
- / (division)
- DIV (integer division)
- MOD (modulus)

Comparison operations

(give a boolean result: true or false)

eg: 456 > 34 is true

- < (less than)
- > (greater than)
- <= (less than or equal to)
- >= (greater than or equal to)
- <> (not equal to)
- = (equal to)

When performing operations on data items you need to consider the data types used. For example, in a simple calculation where two whole numbers are added together, define variables as follows:

```
Var
    Num1, num2, total : integer;
```

But if the calculation involves division then the answer variable must be declared as a real number:

```
Var
    Num1, num2 : integer;
    answer     : real;
```

The arithmetic operators DIV and MOD can only be performed on whole numbers, integers.

DIV is integer division. It works like normal division but returns the whole number of times one number goes into the other. Here are some examples:

   10 DIV 3 = 3   300 DIV 30 = 10   305 DIV 30 = 10

MOD gives the remainder of integer division as follows:

   10 MOD 3 = 1   300 DIV 30 = 0   305 DIV 30 = 5

Boolean Data Type:

Boolean variables are either true or false. It makes no sense to perform mathematical operations on them or to compare them to see which is greater. With boolean variables we use **logical operators** to create **boolean expressions**. (Boolean expressions were used earlier to control loops, we called them conditions.) Logical operations you should know are:

Logical operations			**!!! NB...**
• NOT	• AND	• OR	AND takes precedence over OR

Consider an estate agent's program that searches through a file of house details to find ones that match a customer's requirements:

```
IF (NumberOfRooms>3) AND ((type="House") OR (type="Flat")) THEN
    Display details
END IF
```

The table below summarises the operations that can be performed on each data type.

Integer	Real	Boolean
Arithmetic operations Comparison operations	Arithmetic operations *(but not DIV and MOD, which only apply to whole numbers)* Comparison operations	Logical operations

Arrays

The OCR Specification says that you should be able to:

• use one-dimensional arrays

Earlier in this chapter we talked about variables. If we were processing one or two specific data items, then we would have a variable for each of these. For example, a program that adds two numbers together might use variables called `num1`, `num2` and `total`, all of type integer.

Often a program will process a number of data items of the same type. For example, if a program is processing gas bills for 10,000 people. The basic calculation is the same for each person's bill:

```
GasUsed  x PricePerUnit.
```

We could use variables called GasUsed1, GasUsed2, GasUsed3…GasUsed10000 to store the amount of gas used by each customer but most programming languages allow you to use an **array** to make processing groups of data easier to code. An array is a group of data items of the same data type, which is stored under one identifier (name) in contiguous (one after another) memory locations.

Simple (1-dimentional) Array

This program processes 12 numbers using a simple array called **numbers**. Imagine a table with 1 row of 12 boxes:

Numbers:

1	2	3	4	5	6	7	8	9	10	11	12

Each box in the table can contain an integer. Each box has a numerical reference call a **subscript** that is used to refer to that individual data item. For example, the third box in this array is referred to as:

```
numbers[3]
```

At the start of a program the array will be defined, just as you would a variable. In Delphi or Pascal the array declaration for the array shown above would look like this:

```
numbers : array [1..12] of integer;
```

The individual boxes in the array can be used just like variables:

- **Assign** values to them: `Numbers[4]=27;`
- **Read** values into them from the keyboard or a file:
  `Read(numbers[4]);`
- **Write** the value stored in a box to the screen or a file:
  `Write('The fourth value is ', numbers[4]);`

> !!! NB…
>
> Some languages, such as Java and C++, start numbering arrays zero rather than 1.

The benefits of using arrays are:

- Code is easier to follow and therefore easier to debug and maintain.
- A group of data can be easily processed using a FOR loop.

When you program a group of data in an array we usually end up doing the same thing to each data item so having them stored in numbered locations makes it much easier. The **algorithm** over the page gets 12 numbers from the user, adds them up and outputs the total:

```
total=0  ◄─────────────────────────────────
for loop= 1 to 12 do
    write('Enter number ',loop,': ')
    read(numbers[loop]) ◄───────────────────
    total=total+numbers[loop]
next loop
write('Total is ',total);
```

Initialise the variable, 'total' to zero at the start

Reads each number into the numbered location in the array, based on the value of "loop" each time. Loop=1 the first time, 2 the second time etc

Refers to the current value of loop to add a specific number to the total

ERRORS

The OCR Specification says that you should be able to:

- describe syntax errors and logic errors which may occur while developing a program
- understand and identify syntax and logic errors

When you write a program in a high level programming language a translator (compiler or interpreter, see earlier in chapter) will scan each line of code and convert it into machine code. As you will already have found out, programming is not as easy as it looks! It is very easy to make silly mistakes typing in the code, **syntax errors**, or get the code to run but find out it doesn't actually do what you wanted! These are **logic errors**.

Syntax errors

The translator expects commands to have a certain format, called **syntax**, just like a sentence in English has grammar rules. Syntax is a set of rules that states what each command format must be. For example, in Delphi/Pascal you would define variables in the format:

```
VariableName : Datatype;
```

The compiler knows that this statement must have an identifier followed by a colon, followed by a recognised data type and a semi-colon at the end.

In Visual Basic an IF statement must have this format:

```
IF x=10 THEN
    Grade="Pass"
ELSE
    Grade="Fail"
END IF
```

!!! NB…

If you spell identifiers, such as variable names, incorrectly this is not a problem, as long as you always spell it wrong in the same way!

Without the correct key words the compiler will not be able to translate it into machine code and will give a syntax error.

Some common syntax errors include:

- Mistyping a key word: WRIET instead of WRITE

- Missing key words out of constructs such as starting a REPEAT loop but not writing UNTIL anywhere

- Opening brackets but not closing them

- Not having the right number of parameters inside brackets for functions, for example: `Answer=round(TheNumber)` will give a syntax error if the language expects another parameter to state the number of decimal places: `Answer=round(TheNumber,2)`

A program will not compile and run if there are syntax errors.

Logic errors

Once the code is written correctly, with no syntax errors, the program will compile. The program can then be run. Just because the program will run does not mean that it is working correctly though! Often we run the program and it doesn't do quite what we expected. This is called a **logic error**.

Typical logic errors that you have probably coded already include:

- Missing brackets from mathematical calculations:
  `NetPay=GrossPay-TaxFreePart x TaxRate`
  Is not the same as:
  `NetPay=(GrossPay-TaxFreePart) x TaxRate`

> **!!! NB...**
>
> Remember BIDMAS? Brackets first, then multiply and divide and then add and subtract!

- Loops that do not execute the correct number of times because a condition states X>10 instead of X>=10.

- Variables have not been initialised, or have been initialised in the wrong place (often incorrectly initialised inside the loop instead of just before it).

- Flawed algorithms that just don't do what they were intended to do. Capturing all of the complexities of real-life scenarios in code is difficult and users always manage to do something to the input that you didn't cater for!

Often these logic errors are hard to spot. You should always do a visual check of output to check it isn't ridiculous but you also need to do some systematic testing to make sure the program really does behave as expected (see next section).

TESTING

> The OCR Specification says that you should be able to:
>
> - select and justify test data for a program, stating the expected outcome of each test

How do you know if your program really works? It may run and produce output but you need to check that the output is as expected. If you made a spreadsheet that multiplied pounds by a conversion rate to get dollars you would probably type in an easy number like £10 to see if the number of dollars looked right. We test programs in a similar way. We decide on some sensible test values to put into the program to test that the outputs look as we'd expect.

Planning how to test a program

A good way of planning your testing is to write down what sample data you will use to make sure the program works. This is a "Test Plan". It is important that you think about this before you write the program so you don't move the goalposts later!

You can formalise your plan by using a table with the following headings:

Test purpose	Test data	Expected outcome	Actual outcome

The first three columns are part of our design and planning stage and the final column is completed when we test the finished program

If numbers or dates are being entered by the user then you should use test data that checks both ends of the allowed range as well as data that should not be allowed, just outside this range. This is known as testing **boundary data** or **extremes**.

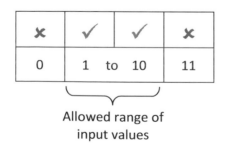

Allowed range of
input values

> !!! NB...
>
> The term "extremes" doesn't mean extremely big or extremely small but refers to the extremes of the range, the smallest and largest values allowed.

The test plan for testing this validation would look like the one shown over page.

Test purpose	Test data	Expected outcome
1. Check user can only enter number between 1 and 10	1 *(lowest valid number)*	Input is accepted
2. Check user can only enter number between 1 and 10	10 *(highest valid number)*	Input is accepted
3. Check user can only enter number between 1 and 10	0 *(not allowed)*	User gets and error message and asked to enter number again
4. Check user can only enter number between 1 and 10	11 *(not allowed)*	User gets and error message and asked to enter number again
5. Check user can only enter number between 1 and 10	5 *(typical number)*	Input accepted
6. Check user can only enter number between 1 and 10	? *(non-numerical entries not allowed)*	User gets and error message and asked to enter number again

If text is being entered check what happens when you enter nothing or a string that is too long, as well as the text you would expect to be ok.

Test purpose	Test data	Expected outcome
7. Check user password works	"Frogs" *(correct password)*	User allowed to continue
8. Check user password works	"cats" *(incorrect password)*	Error message and asked to try again
9. Check user password works	"" *(no password)*	Error message and asked to try again

IDE TOOLS

- describe common tools and facilities available in an integrated development environment (IDE): editors, error diagnostics, run-time environment, translators, auto-documentation

When you create a program you will be using a software package that helps you write the code more easily. This is called an **Integrated Development Environment** or **IDE.**

The screenshot below shows the form design view in the Delphi 2007 IDE. The key features labeled are common to most IDEs.

A list of all the properties for the currently-selected component, where their values can be set. For example, setting the font and colour of a text box.

A list of all the components within the project that can be referenced in the code. This makes it easy for the programmer to see all of the objects on the form and how they were named.

An overview of the program files that make up a "project" or system. A project may consist of many different forms, all connected together.

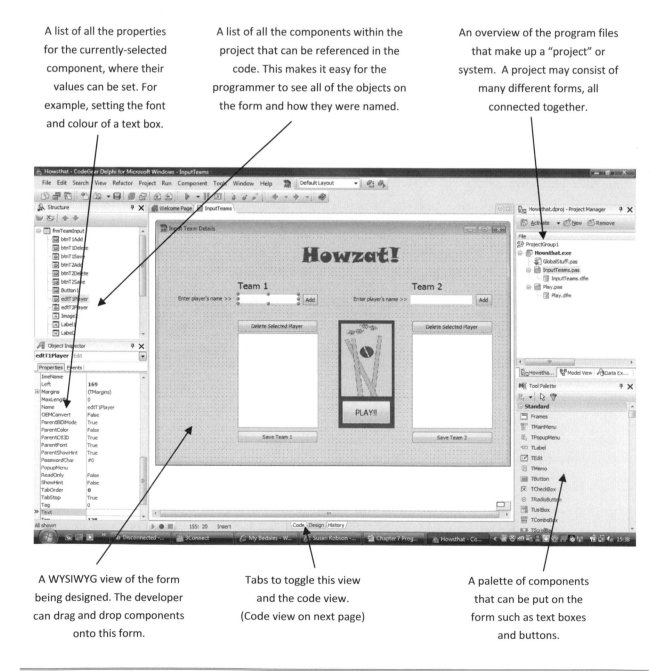

A WYSIWYG view of the form being designed. The developer can drag and drop components onto this form.

Tabs to toggle this view and the code view. (Code view on next page)

A palette of components that can be put on the form such as text boxes and buttons.

Editing Environment

When you write the code the IDE will provide helpful features in the editing environment such as colour-coding key words, numbering the lines and even auto-completing constructs for you.

The line numbers make it easy to see which bit of code an error message relates to. The auto-completion of constructs reduces errors such as missing "ends" or starting a "repeat" loop and forgetting the "until" part.

Run-time Environment

When you run the program the IDE will provide the translator, in this case a compiler, needed to run the program. The screen and the feedback you see when you try to run the program are provided by the **run-time environment**.

When you try to compile the program the IDE will generate error messages in a diagnostics window. Notice how the IDE has highlighted the line in red. This is the line causing the error and the message below that says, "Missing operator or semicolon".

As well as assisting the programmer with error messages there are other debugging tools that allow the programmer to stop the program running at a certain line (called a **breakpoint**) and allows them to check the values of certain variables. This is a very useful debugging tool.

In this case there is a breakpoint at line 20 so the programmer can hover over a variable before that point to see what value a variable has. Here you can see that "choice" has the value 3. Sometimes the value isn't what you'd expect!

Translators

When the code has been written it must be translated into machine code before it can run. An IDE includes the translators that will either compile or interpret the code, as required (see p113-114, for an explanation of the different translators). The compiler will check the syntax and report any errors. The program will compile fully once all the syntax errors have been removed. The Compiler can then convert the high-level programming code into machine code.

Auto-Documentation

When a developer writes the code it is good practice to use comments in the code. The compiler recognises comment lines because they start with a special symbol. For example:

```
//   This is a comment in a Delphi program
'    This is a comment in a Visual Basic program
<!-- This is a comment in HTML -->
```

These comments can then be used to create program documentation automatically.

The IDE takes a note of all the variables, modules and sub-routines as the project is developed. The compiler uses this data along with the developer's comments to generate a text file that can be the basis of the programmer's technical documentation. Technical documentation is important when the program is maintained.

GLOSSARY OF TERMS

Algorithms

Algorithm	A series of steps to solve a problem. Can be expressed in structured English, pseudocode or as a system flowchart.
System Flow Chart	A diagram using commonly defined symbols to express and algorithm.
Structured English	A way of writing an algorithm in natural language using some basic programming constructs such as IF...THEN...ELSE and loops. More structured than just natural language/prose.
Pseudocode	A way of writing an algorithm that is close to actual programming language, using coding-style constructs such as IF...THEN...ELSE, loops and array notation as appropriate.
Hungarian Notation	The convention of prefixing identifiers to indicate what type of object they are. Commonly used with forms where, for example the prefix *txt* might indicate a textbox and *lst* might prefix a list box. The prefix is conventionally in lowercase.
camelCase	The use of capital letters in an identifier to make them more readable. With camelCase the first word is not capitalised: `txtCustomer, lstCounty, frmAddCustomer, btnSubmit`
PascalCase	The use of capital letters in an identifier to make it more readable. For example, variable and procedure identifiers: `StudentNumber, ProductID, StartPoint, CalcTotal`
Sequence	Where instructions are executed one after another in series.
Selection	Where the program will execute certain instructions based on conditions. Selection statements include: IF...THEN...ELSE and CASE...OF to select which commands to execute.
Iteration	Where a program will execute a group of instructions zero or more times based on a condition. FOR loops will execute instructions a specific number of times, REPEAT...UNTIL loops for one or more times and WHILE...DO loops for zero or more time.
Condition	A boolean expression that controls an iteration or selection statement. For example, `REPEAT...UNTIL X=10` (`X=10` is the condition).
Boolean expression	An expression that is true or false. For example: `continue="Y"` Expressions can be more complex, containing several parts: `((continue="Y") or (continue="y"))and (tries<10)`

Programming languages

High level programming language	A programming language where programming constructs are written in a way that is close to natural language instead of in mnemonics or machine code such as Delphi, Pascal, Visual Basic, Java, C++ etc.
Assembly language	2nd generation programming language where instructions are in the form of mnemonics.
Mnemonics	A way of writing programming instructions using abbreviations of commands and the data to be used. For example: LDA #34, ADD &5F3A
Machine code	1st generation code, binary instructions where some bits are used to define the operation (opcode) and some bits define the data to be used.
Translator	The piece of systems software used to convert different programming languages into machine code. Three types: assembler, interpreter and compiler.
Interpreter	A translator that converts high level languages into machine code. Works one line at a time checking syntax, converting to machine code and executing the code.
Compiler	A translator that converts high level languages into machine code. Works through the whole program (source code) checking the syntax, then converting to machine code and creating the executable object code. The object code is executed, not the source code.
Source code	The original high level program.
Object code	The executable version of the program after it has been compiled.
Assembler	The translator that converts assembly language programs into machine code.

Handling Data in Algorithms

Identifier	A unique name for something (variable, constant, program, procedure etc) within the program.
Constant	A named value within a program that is assigned a specific value. Its value does not change while the program is running.
Variable	An identifier associated with a particular memory location, used to store data. Its value may change as the program is run and new values are assigned to it.
Data type	A formal description of the type of data being stored in a variable. It defines the amount of memory required and the type of operations that can be performed on that variable.

Handling Data in Algorithms (continued)

Integer	Data type for whole numbers, typically 2 bytes.
Real	Data type for fractional numbers, typically 4 bytes.
Char	Data type for a single character, 1 byte.
String	Data type for text, more than one character. Usually up to 255 characters and takes 1 byte per character.
Boolean	True or false. Typically 1 byte.
Operations	The actions that can be performed on a variable.
Arithmetic operations	Add, subtract, multiply, divide, integer division (DIV) and modulus (MOD)
Comparison operations	= < > <= >= <>
Logical operators	NOT AND OR
Boolean expressions	Expressions that resolve to true or false such as x<=20
Array	A group of data items of the same data type that use a single identifier. Individual data items are accessed using a subscript.

Errors and Testing

Syntax	A set of rules that defines how program statements must be written in order for the translator to understand them
Syntax errors	An error in the format of the program statements such as missing semicolons or keywords spelt incorrectly
Logic errors	An error in the algorithm that means the outcome is not as expected, even though the program will run
Valid data	Data that should be allowed by the program. For example, if a range of 1 to 10 is allowed, then valid data will be any number between 1 and 10 inclusive.
Invalid data	Data that is not valid and should be rejected by the program. For example, if a range of 1 to 10 is allowed, then invalid data will include -251, 0, 11 and 345.
Boundary data	Data either side of the range extremes. For example in a range of 1 to 10 boundary data will include 0, 1, 10 and 11

PAST EXAM QUESTIONS & EXAMPLE ANSWERS

From the specimen paper

8 A program includes the following code.

```
If A > B Then
A = B
B = A
End If
```

(a) The code uses the variables A and B.

Describe what is meant by a variable.

An identifier in a program that names a location in memory where data is stored while being used in a program. Its value can be changed as the program runs.

[2]

(b) State the final values of the variables A and B if the values at the beginning of the code are

A = 4 B = 9

Final value of A = *4*

Final value of B = *9*

A = 6 B = 2

Final value of A = *2*

Final value of B = *2*

NB: Once A takes the value of B then they both have the same value!! The original value of A is lost.

[2]

(c) The intention of lines 02 and 03 is to swap the contents of the variables A and B. This does not work.

Rewrite the code so that the contents of the variables are swapped correctly.

If A > B Then

C = A

A = B

B = C

End If

NB: To swap two things over in memory you always need a third, temporary location to save the value of one of them in!!

[3]

From the specimen paper

12   A display board can show a flashing message of up to 20 characters.

(a) A program allows users to input the message to be displayed and the number of times it
     should flash.

     State the data type of each item of the input data.

     Message: *string*   [1]

     Number of flashes: *integer*   [1]

(b) Write an algorithm for the program that:

     •   Allows the user to input the message and the number of flashes

     •   Rejects the message if it is longer than 20 characters and stops

     •   Otherwise it repeatedly displays the message and clears the display for the correct
         number of times.

```
Begin
    Input Message
    Input NumberOfFlashes
    If length(Message) > 20 Then
        Output "This message is too long"
    Else
        For i = 1 to NumberOfFlashes
            Display Message
            Wait
            Clear Message
            Wait
        Next i
    End If
End
```

*NB: The pauses (wait) are a nice touch
but you'd still have got all the marks
as long as you had a loop that flashed
the correct number of time.*   [5]

8   A syntax error can occur when writing a program.

(a)   State what is meant by a syntax error, giving an example.

An error in the code where it does not meet the grammar rules for that language. For example, "While x=3" without the word "do" at the end or a misspelt keyword like "wriet" instead of "write".   [2]

(b)   Describe tools and facilities available in an integrated development environment (IDE) that can help the programmer to identify and correct syntax errors.

When writing code the IDE will flag up syntax errors. There is a diagnostics window where errors are listed with line numbers to show where they are. Also errors such as unrecognised variables are underlined in the code.

When you compile the code the compiler will generate error messages and highlight the line where the problem has occurred.

The IDE provides editing facilities so the code can be corrected. Many standard word processing editing commands work in the IDE such as copy, paste, find and replace etc   [4]

NB: To maximize marks on a question like this you must notice all of the parts to the question. Here you must mention how errors can be identified as well as how they can be corrected.

Also, notice that my answer talks about errors being identified when the code is written as well as when it is compiled.

Some key words and phrases have been shown in bold. It is important to use the technical terms if you can remember them.